The Book of Pets

Everything you've ever wanted to know about all kinds of pets. Whether you want a lizard, a canary, a monkey, or a dog or cat, this book will help you be a better pet owner. You'll find out about the cost, care, feeding, housing, and breeding of different pets, and also whether you're suited to a particular kind of pet. In order to be able to take really good care of your pet, learn about the sicknesses various pets get and how to treat them. Owning a pet is a grand experience—being responsible for another living thing's care and welfare is a big part of the enjoyment.

So, before you go out and buy that guinea pig, read *The Book of Pets.* Maybe you're more the saltwater fish type!

THE BOOK OF Pets

Stanley Leinwoll

JULIAN MESSNER
New York

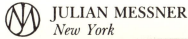

To Rita and Irv

Library of Congress Cataloging in Publication Data

Leinwoll, Stanley.
The book of pets.

Bibliography: p.
Includes index.
SUMMARY: Provides information about the cost, care,
feeding, breeding, and housing of the most popular
pets.
1. Pets—Juvenile literature. [1. Pets]
I. Title
SF416.2.L44   636.08'87   80-17598
ISBN 0-671-33071-3

ACKNOWLEDGMENT

I wish to thank my wife, Miriam, who, as usual, read my manuscript and made many valuable suggestions. I am also indebted to Lorraine Littman Heine, who typed *The Book of Pets* and helped bring order out of chaos. The Park Pet Center of Kendall Park, New Jersey, was very helpful, as well as patient, permitting us to disturb some of its beautiful pets for long and sometimes tedious photo sessions.

CONTENTS

1
SO YOU WANT TO HAVE A PET?

A pet is a living creature that we bring into our home to care for and enjoy. It becomes a member of the family. Like young children with their parents, pets can become almost totally dependent on their owners for food, shelter, care, and in many cases, love. As a matter of fact, many pets will not thrive in the home unless they get love and attention. Having a pet can be a beautiful and rewarding experience, but it is also a responsibility. It is important to realize that the pleasures you can gain from keeping a pet are directly related to the time and energy you are willing to devote to it.

Just about every one of us has a need to love and be loved, and probably the principal reason most people keep pets is to satisfy this need. Some animals are more loving than others. Dogs, cats, monkeys, and even rodents can become very attached to their owners. Birds such as parakeets, parrots, and mynahs will also become attached to those who care for them. Canaries, on the other hand, won't. But a canary has many other redeeming features: male canaries are capable of singing beautifully and are a

9

joy to have around the house. Most canaries are colorful
as well, and the combination of bright colors and brilliant
song accounts for the popularity of these lovely birds.
Fish, on the other hand, neither show love nor sing. Yet
keeping fish in the home is a source of great pleasure to
millions of hobbyists. There are many reasons for this.
Fish are quiet, clean, and easy to keep. They never
scratch up the furniture or bite the mailman. A well-main-
tained aquarium with plants and rocks is pleasant to watch
and can provide hours of peaceful relaxation. Most
aquarium fish can be bred easily and kept for many years
with a minimum of trouble. Many of the most interesting
aquarium fish are inexpensive, as well.

Some fish have very unusual breeding habits. There is
a group, for example, that bears its young live; watching
a female give birth is an unforgettable experience, as is
watching certain egg layers in action.

Many fish are brilliantly colored, and one can spend
hours virtually hypnotized in front of a tank watching
these beauties cutting gracefully, silently, through the water.

Keeping a pet can satisfy the artistic instincts of many
of us. Whether it's an aquarium or a terrarium, it is very
satisfying to create an attractive environment of rocks,
plants, gravel, and, where appropriate, wood. Whether
the motif is a desert landscape for a snake or a tropical
setting for a reptile, arranging the habitat can be great fun
and a continuing source of enjoyment.

There is much to be learned from keeping pets. Dogs,
cats, fish, rodents, and some birds and reptiles will breed
in the home. Determining optimal conditions under which
various species breed best is an education in itself, and
interested pet owners can and should learn about the
native habitats of their pets, optimal temperature range,
best humidity conditions, and eating habits. How

much and what you learn depends only on the amount of time and effort you are willing to devote to your pet. Pets can be of great therapeutic value. Recent medical studies have shown that people who are ill recover more rapidly, and in cases of serious illness have a higher survival rate, if they have pets. The psychological implications of these studies have not been fully evaluated as yet, but it stands to reason that the will to live may be connected with recovery from illness. A person who has a pet to care for and love may be more motivated to survive than someone who doesn't.

Animals can be great companions, loving and very attentive to their owners, and the owners should reciprocate. If pet owners do not have the time to give, they are doing themselves as well as their animals an injustice.

Having a pet means assuming a responsibility, whether to maintain a fish tank by feeding the fish daily and cleaning the tank when necessary, or to expend the time and energy required to train a dog and give it the attention and affection it needs in order to thrive.

Unfortunately, many people do not consider the future when they take a pet into their home. Many commitments to a pet are made on the spur of the moment, without consideration of the amount of time, effort, energy, and money that must go into the care and rearing of some house pets. Animals such as cats, dogs, and rodents regularly produce offspring, and although seeing your pet through its pregnancy can be an informative and wondrous experience, all too often poor planning makes it necessary to dispose of excess pets by destroying them. Proper planning would make it unnecessary to do away with these creatures.

Animals grow up. A cute, cuddly golden retriever pup grows into a large animal that requires a great deal of attention. Although adorable when small, a retriever is not a lapdog. A cairn terrier is a lapdog. It will learn to play ball, and mine can take the lid off a can of tennis balls, get them out of the can, and bring them to me in its mouth. But cairns bark a lot, never tire of playing, and want to have their bellies rubbed just about all the time. If they are not given attention, they brood and sulk. It is important to know these things about a potential pet beforehand, lest an animal be neglected later. Frequently an owner discovers too late how much time and attention a pet needs, and the result is almost always sad. Neglected animals are unhappy animals.

A teething puppy will chew on the furniture and before it has been trained will probably urinate and defecate in the house. Are you prepared for that? Cats are easier to housebreak, but they have a tendency to scratch the furniture.

Remember also that some animals live a long time. A friend of mine has a cat who is eighteen years old. Although most cats don't live that long, pet owners must be prepared to make a long-term commitment to their pets. Some pets can live twenty or thirty years or more. Do you want to keep a pet that long?

Cost is another factor to consider when you choose a pet. Although the initial expense of becoming a pet owner may be minimal (for example, a friend may give you a dog or cat), there are inevitable expenses involved. Animals have to be fed every day. When they are ill they must receive special attention. This may mean something as simple as purchasing medicine in a pet store, or something more complex like taking the animal to a veterinarian and paying for treatment.

If your animal lives in a cage, you will want to clean its home thoroughly at least once a week. That means removing the animal and keeping it in a deep pail or bucket or in another cage while you do the housework.

This requires removing everything, including the nesting box, all bedding material, and naturally food particles and droppings as well. A stainless steel cage, although somewhat more expensive than a glass aquarium, is a practical investment because it is easiest to keep clean and maintain. Most pet shops stock a range of cages, whose cost will vary according to the size and the materials they are made of.

Keeping the cage clean makes pet-keeping more pleasant in the long run, because a dirty cage starts to smell before long, and you don't want that. Even more important than the smell, however, is the fact that the health of your pet can depend on cleanliness. Bacteria breed more readily in dirt, and the cleaner and neater the cage, the better off your pet will be. When the cage is cleaned, it should routinely be disinfected to discourage mites, lice, fleas, flies, and other disease carriers. Pet shops normally stock cage disinfectants, and these should be used according to the directions on the label. You needn't disinfect the cage every time you clean. As a general rule, about once every six weeks in the late fall, winter, and early spring is satisfactory. In the warmer months, every two to three weeks is advisable.

Knowing in advance the kind of care your pet will need and how much it will cost you to provide it is one of the objectives of this book. We will try to provide you with enough information to enable you to get the most enjoyment from the pet of your choosing, and to help you determine whether the pet you are interested in is suited to your needs. It is not sufficient simply to "love animals."

This book will provide, in simple language, information about the cost, care, feeding, breeding, and housing of the most popular pets. Because of space limitations, not all possible pets will be discussed. We will generally confine ourselves to those that are small enough to be kept in a home. Thus, domestic animals such as cows, pigs, and horses will not be included.

An easy-reference table in the back of the book summarizes the most important facts about each of the pets covered in the book.

2
RODENTS

GENERAL INFORMATION

Probably the first animals to come to mind when one mentions pets are dogs and cats. Mention rodents and many people cringe. Unfortunately, they associate rodents with field mice and rats and all the unpleasant images most people have of them—disease-carrying, dirty, dangerous. Yet many rodents are easy to keep, great fun to have around, and fascinating to watch. Among rodents most frequently kept as pets are many strains of mice, white rats, gerbils, hamsters, and guinea pigs.

All of these animals have certain things in common: they are small, curious, very active, and should be housed in cages. They can, of course, be removed from the cages and played with, but they must not be allowed to get far out of reach. A pair of hamsters I had some years ago got away while my children were playing with them and disappeared from sight. We looked high and low but couldn't find them. Months later, we found their remains while we were cleaning out our heating system. They had made their way into the vents, which were in the foundation of our house, and were unable to find their way out. I never

15

told my children. We also kept turning up evidence of places in the house they had been. Hamsters, like many rodents, build nests of almost anything soft and fluffy, and they apparently discovered that the upholstery of our living room furniture made great bedding.

Mice must also be watched carefully. A family we had (mother, father, and six offspring) escaped from their cages one evening, and we were unable to find them. Since mice breed at a furious clip, my wife and I were concerned that in a short time, if our pets were not found, the house would be overrun. We were desperate and even considered setting traps for them, but we couldn't bring ourselves to do it. Aware that mice are nocturnal, for several nights we set food out late at night, after making certain the rest of the house was spotless, and kept a vigil in our kitchen. One by one the mice came out. Since they were tame, having been handled gently by all of us at one time or another, we were able to round them up.

Metal cages are essential for rodents, because they gnaw and can chew their way through a wooden cage in no time. Rodent cages should have wire mesh floors and a removable tray below the floor to facilitate daily cleaning.

Like humans, rodents like their privacy and should be given a place to which they can retreat. Ideally, a small metal or plastic box should be used. Rodents also need bedding material in the cage. Just about anything soft and absorbent will do—wood chips, shredded paper, cat litter, cotton, or small pieces of fabric.

If you have a glass fish tank, it can be used to house a rodent, provided the tank is large enough. As a general rule, the cage or tank should be at least four times the length of your pet so it will have adequate room to move around. The chief disadvantage to using a glass aquarium is that it does not have a removable bottom or wire mesh floor. This makes cleaning more difficult. Furthermore, if you do use an aquarium, you need a cover to fit across the entire top, either of wire mesh or metal. Rodents have an insatiable appetite to escape and will crawl, climb, jump, or do whatever is necessary to get out.

The temperature at which rodents are kept is fairly important. In general, a range of about 65 to 80 degrees fahrenheit is optimal. (All temperatures in this book are given in degrees fahrenheit.) Your pets will tolerate greater ranges, but the further the temperature is from the optimum, the less they will like it.

Although not quite as crucial, humidity is also a factor which influences the well-being of rodents. If the humidity goes above 60 percent for long periods of time, the danger of respiratory infection is increased.

It is most important to obtain a pet that is in good health. The chances are, with a rodent, that you will get it from a friend or from a pet shop. If a friend gives you your animal, make its health a condition of acceptance. A sick animal is listless, its eyes are dull and glassy, and its coat is dull. Don't let a friend talk you into taking a sick animal. If you purchase the animal from a pet shop, get a guarantee that you can return it within a week if it turns out to be ill. Take your time in buying. Before purchasing, watch the animal a while. Be certain that it is active and that its appetite is good. It should not scratch itself excessively. One of the major problems with purchasing a rodent at a pet shop is mites and lice. You can generally get a feeling about a pet shop from the way the cages are kept. They should be clean and odor-free. All the animals should be healthy looking. Don't rush. You may be eager to take a particular animal home, but it is better to be patient than sorry.

All rodents are primarily vegetarians. Some will eat meat, and rats and mice love bacon, but rodents do best on a diet of seeds, grasses, nuts, and some fruits and vegetables. In addition, commercial foods, consisting either of pellets or of seed mixtures, are available for all rodents. Some rodents have special nutritional requirements. Guinea pigs must have vitamin C in their diet or they will get scurvy. Most pet shops selling guinea pigs will also sell special pellets containing this vitamin.

For humans, variety is the spice of life. Although this may not be quite so true for your pet, remember that by varying its diet you will make its life more interesting. You can try carrots, lettuce, celery, apples, seeds, cereals, potatoes, and bread, supplemented with pellet food or even dog kibble. You can also try table scraps. Experience will be your best teacher. In the summer, offer your pet fresh grasses and dandelion leaves. But go easy when introducing new food. Rodents are very susceptible to diarrhea induced by changes in diet. This is not good either for your pet or for you.

With the exception of guinea pigs, which have a tendency to make pigs of themselves and are prone to overeat, your rodents should have access to food all the time, because they are nibblers by nature.

All rodents need water. Since they are very active and not terribly smart, water in a dish is soon overturned. About the only practical way to meet their need is with a gravity-flow bottle. These are available in most pet shops.

As has been said earlier, rodents are gnawing animals, and it is necessary to keep something in the cage they can gnaw on, like a piece of hardwood. As an alternative, try a beef bone, which also contains minerals, or hard-shelled nuts, such as brazil nuts, hazelnuts, or black walnuts. Which of the above your pet prefers to sharpen his teeth on will depend on the animal.

Some last general words about rodents. Most rodents make friendly, gentle pets. They enjoy being handled and petted and will respond very well to such treatment. But because they are naturally timid, you should be very careful about how you handle them when you first bring them home. It is a good idea to leave the animal alone for a few days so it can get accustomed to its new surroundings. After that, try to coax your pet out of its cage into your hand. Perhaps a morsel of food will help.

Don't make any sudden gestures if you can avoid it and be very gentle. Most animals will bite if they are frightened, and although there is little or no danger of infection from a domestic rodent, it is no fun being bitten. Once your pet gets to know you, it is not likely to bite you.

Some rodents breed very quickly. Watching a mother give birth and raise her young is fascinating as well as educational. Remember that when the young mature they will need cages of their own, unless you have made arrangements to sell them or give them away. Whatever you decide, do a little planning in advance so you won't have to do away with a litter of unwanted animals.

With these generalities taken care of, we can discuss in more detail those rodents most commonly raised as pets.

MICE

Mice learned to share the human's home (mostly as an uninvited guest) many thousands of years ago. Because they are such prolific breeders and because of their genetic makeup, it has been possible to develop a wide variety of colors and shapes, as well as some that behave peculiarly.

In addition to the more common white mice, blue, red, silver, cream, black, and lilac strains exist. There are mice that have pink eyes, and others with black eyes. Some are spotted, others come in two, three, or more colors. There are mice with wavy hair, with silky hair, and even mice that waltz. These mice have a hereditary inner ear defect which affects their balance, causing them to spend a good deal of time on their hind legs whirling around in circles, giving the illusion of dancing.

The cost of a mouse depends on the variety you choose. You can buy a white mouse for a few dollars. The fancy varieties cost more, but if you plan to breed and sell your pets, they will prove to be the better investment because they will bring a better price. In general, they all cost the same to feed and care for.

Housing

Almost anything will do for housing for mice. Ready-made cages complete with exercise wheels are available in most pet shops. You can use a glass aquarium or even a large jar. Whatever you use, remember that mice are climbers as well as jumpers, and the container must have a tight-fitting cover. If you cover a jar, put air holes in it so the mice can breathe. Mice are active, and the roomier the housing the better. You can provide them with toys such as ladders, treadmills, and trapezes—the more the merrier, and the more fun it will be to watch your pet perform.

A typical rodent cage. The ladder and wheel make life more interesting, and the gravity flow bottle at the lower left enables the animal to drink without spilling the water.

Mice like to burrow and should be provided with nesting material and a nesting box, preferably of metal or plastic, into which they can retreat for privacy. This nesting area should not be disturbed, except for cleaning.

Nesting material can be sawdust, cat litter, wood shavings, pieces of paper toweling, or rags. Do not use newspaper because newsprint could be harmful to mice. Mice usually defecate in the place furthest away from where they sleep, and this area should be cleaned every day or every other day. The entire cage should be thoroughly cleaned once a week, and more often in warm weather.

Feeding

You can get away with feeding mice only rabbit pellets, which contain all the nutrients mice need to survive. But for maximum longevity (a healthy mouse can live three or four years in captivity) and fertility, a varied diet is necessary. This should include fresh vegetables, such as carrots and peas; birdseed (parakeet seed is ideal); grains such as oats; and, as an occasional special treat, a piece of cheese or bacon. Don't give these goodies to your mouse too often or you will have an obese pet in your house.

Other foods that mice enjoy are grasses; particular favorites are timothy hay, clover, and dandelion leaves. These should be given sparingly because they can cause diarrhea. Still another treat for mice is an occasional small piece of white bread soaked in whole milk.

Try all of these and see which are your mouse's favorites.

Mice must have water, and although much of the fluid they require is taken in with their solid food, water should be available at all times. It is not advisable to put containers of water on the floor of the cage. Use a gravity-flow feed bottle. This is a small bottle with a nozzle attachment that is hung on the cage. When your mouse is thirsty, it takes a sip from the nozzle.

Mice are nocturnal: they generally sleep during the day and are most active at night. It is therefore best to feed them their perishables (vegetables, bread soaked in milk, grasses) in the evening. Throw away any uneaten food every morning.

Because their teeth grow constantly, it is necessary to have something for mice to gnaw on at all times. Otherwise, they would soon have unwieldy fangs. Nuts in the shell or beef bones are best.

Breeding

If you do not intend to breed your mice, females make better pets than males because they are virtually odorless and do not exude that familiar mousy odor that males have. To determine the sex of a mouse, simply pick it up and turn it over. If it is a male it will have a tiny penis a short distance in front of the vent. Do not pick a mouse up by the tip of the tail. Rather, take the tail between the thumb and forefinger about half an inch from the vent. An alternative method of picking up a mouse is to take it gently between your thumb and forefinger, holding it behind its front legs. Mice like to be held and petted, and once they are accustomed to you, they will climb all over you looking for bits of food.

A female mouse (called a doe) is ready to breed at the age of two months. The gestation period is about three weeks, and she is ready to breed again within a day after she has had her first litter. Once she has started nursing, however, she cannot conceive until the litter has been weaned. If you want to breed a pair of mice, it is necessary to provide a separate metal or plastic box for them with plenty of nesting material. You will know a doe is pregnant by her swollen teats and enlarged abdomen. Once you are certain the doe is pregnant, the male should be removed. He's of no further use, and you don't want the female pregnant again the day she has her litter. Feed her well. A pregnant female should be fed fresh food twice daily. Once she has her litter, don't disturb the box unless it is absolutely essential. Does have been known to kill their offspring after they had been disturbed by humans.

On the average, the size of the litter will be about six, although some litters are much larger. It has been calculated that one young active pair of mice could produce a total of over thirty thousand descendants in one year if all the offspring of all mice proved to be fertile and healthy. It's awesome to think about!

At birth, mice look like tiny piglets, pink and without fur. Their eyes are shut and they cannot see. Within two weeks, they grow fur, their eyes open, and they are able to crawl about.

One additional word about breeding. Although the young should not be disturbed, it will be necessary to check the litter and remove any dead babies at once. After they have begun to grow, it is a good idea to destroy any defective or deformed mice. The quickest, most humane way is to put a few drops of chloroform on a piece of cotton and put it to the mouse's face.

Ailments

If you are careful about keeping your mouse well fed and its cage clean, chances are its health will remain good. Mice do not have to be bathed. They groom themselves. If room temperature is maintained, they should be free of disease throughout their lifetime. Unfortunately, pets do sometimes become ill, and the treatment will depend on the illness. If a mouse shows symptoms such as loss of fur, loss of fur color, wheezing, loss of appetite, or severe loss of weight, it should immediately be separated from any other mice. Keep it warm, preferably at about 85 degrees. Put a few drops of sweet red wine on a cube of sugar and try to give it to your pet. Try warm whole milk administered with a medicine dropper. If recovery is not rapid and if you are attached to your pet, call a veterinarian. If you are not particularly attached to your pet, the animal should be destroyed before your other pets become infected.

Mice are susceptible to fleas and mites. Frequent scratching is one symptom. Treatment includes a thorough cleaning of the cage, replacement of all bedding, and the use of a commercial flea and mite powder, which can be purchased at most pet stores. Cat flea powder is also effective.

Diarrhea is usually caused by a change in diet, often in the form of greens or vegetables that the animal has not had before or is getting too much of. Dandelion greens, for example, are a great treat but are a frequent cause of stomach upset when fed in excess. If your mouse gets diarrhea, it will usually be associated with a newly added food.

RATS

It is unfortunate that many people have preconceived notions about rats. It is true that wild rats actually are destructive, dangerous, and carriers of many diseases. If we call someone a rat, we are not paying him or her a compliment.

On the other hand, domesticated rats make wonderful pets. Over the years, breeders have developed gentle, interesting, bright, and affectionate little animals.

Essentially, rats and mice are similar, but there are two important differences. Rats are bigger and they are smarter. Many are as smart as most dogs or cats. Rats can be taught to run complicated mazes and to solve difficult problems in reasoning. Domestic rats can easily be tamed and will crawl into your hand when you hold it in front of them. You can teach them to walk on their hind legs by holding a favorite morsel of food above their heads. The quickest way to tame a rat is to hand-feed it and hold it often. It will respond by remaining close by, even when it is out of its cage, and will even follow you as you move about.

Buy your pet rat from a reliable pet shop. There are numerous types and colors available, but white rats generally make the best pets. The cage you keep it in will naturally have to be larger than what you would use for a mouse. Feeding, breeding, and general care are the same as for mice.

In many respects, particularly when it comes to eating, rats are like humans. They will eat just about anything, regardless of whether or not it is good for them. For example, rats love ice cream and beer, but a diet of these will soon produce a rat that looks as if it had been inflated. As a special treat, or if you are training your pet, you can offer small amounts of these treats. But for a regular diet, stick to nuts, vegetables, seeds, grasses, and milk-soaked

A white rat. (*Patricia F. Fishtein*)

One of the many interesting varieties of rat that has been developed by breeders. The one shown is brown and white. (*Patricia F. Fishtein*)

bread. You can experiment with other foods, but do so in moderation.

GERBILS

Not too long ago, gerbils (pronounced JER bulls) were considered exotic pets and were very expensive to purchase. They were introduced to America from Mongolia about twenty-five years ago. In all, a total of twenty-two were brought in, and every gerbil in the country is a descendent of these original animals.

A grown gerbil is larger than a mouse, smaller than a rat, and weighs about 3 ounces. It has a long, furry tail, black-tipped light brown fur, large bulging eyes, and large ears. Its hind legs are longer than its forelegs, and it hops like a rabbit.

Gerbils are diurnal; they sleep at night and confine their activity to the daytime. Given enough nesting materials, gerbils dig elaborate retreats into which they burrow. Like other rodents, gerbils must have something to gnaw on and are happiest when they have ladders, exercise wheels, and treadmills so that they can stay active. Like mice and rats, they can be kept in a cage or a properly outfitted aquarium.

Gerbils eat what rats and mice do—seeds, grains, vegetables, some fruits, nuts, and grasses. Sweet hay is a special treat, as are the seeds of sunflowers, pumpkins, and watermelons. Birdseed mixtures for canaries and parakeets are also welcomed with relish, as are pieces of apple, corn, oats, and barley.

Coming from the desert as they do, gerbils require little water. Most of the water they need is obtained from moist fruits and vegetables; nevertheless, a gravity-flow bottle should be part of the paraphernalia kept in the cage. Because gerbils drink very little, they urinate very little, and consequently their cages are relatively easy to keep clean.

Gerbils are very hardy and comparatively disease-free. They have a tendency to get diarrhea when overfed or when a new food is introduced into their diet. This can be remedied by eliminating the new food. Although gerbils can tolerate wide temperature ranges, they should be kept out of drafts and, if possible, protected from high humidity.

Although gerbils are very tame, they will bite if frightened. They should be handled gently and abrupt movements should be avoided. They can be trained to eat from your hand and enjoy being held and played with.

Gerbils should not be bathed. They spend hours grooming themselves. Like many other furry creatures, they are sometimes attacked by lice and mites. The best prevention for this is a clean cage. If lice or mites become a problem, buy a powder sold for cats. Gerbils, like cats, lick themselves, so only nontoxic powders can be used.

Gerbils are very social and should be with other gerbils.

Don't buy fewer than two. They are monogamous and mate for life. If a mate dies, don't introduce another one right away. It is best to separate the new pair with a wire mesh so that they can become accustomed to the new scent. Although gerbils do not breed as rapidly as rats and mice, their rate of reproduction is formidable. Unless you are breeding for sale purposes, it is probably better to keep pairs of the same sex together.

The gestation period of gerbils is about three and a half weeks, and the average litter is five. The young are weaned at six weeks and mature at twelve, at which time they are ready to pair off and start families of their own. If you are breeding gerbils, pairs should be separated from the others and placed in cages of their own as soon as they mature.

Gerbil cubs are born without fur and are blind for the first three weeks. They should be disturbed as little as possible after birth, and the mother treated very gently. If frightened, she may move the babies to another location or eat them.

In captivity a well-cared-for gerbil can live for about four years. A mated pair will stop producing after two or two and a half years but will remain affectionate toward each other until they die. I had a very devoted pair for four years. They were inseparable. Finally, the female died. Attempts to put other gerbils in with the brooding male were of no avail. He sulked, ate little, and died within a month. It was very sad to watch. I am sure he died of a broken heart.

HAMSTERS

The word *hamster* comes from the German, *hamstern*, to hoard. Anyone who has seen a hamster with its cheek pouches filled to capacity knows how appropriate this

A golden hamster begging for food. (*Patricia F. Fishtein*)

name is. Hamsters stuff these pouches with food or nesting materials, then run off to store the hoard in a secure place.

The golden hamster, the most common of the hamsters raised as pets, was discovered in Syria in 1930. All the millions of hamsters now raised in this country are descended from an original find consisting of a mother and twelve offspring.

Although the golden hamster is available in various colors, the most common one is golden-brown with white or grayish markings on the underside and a small, stumpy tail. Its eyes are black and bulging (except for albinos, which have pink eyes), and it looks very much like a tiny bear.

Of all the pets in the rodent family, hamsters are most likely to bite, and have a reputation for being mean. Purchasing a hamster in a pet shop, therefore, should be a leisurely, carefully planned activity. If a potential pet appears skittish, runs from you when offered food, or tries to bite when you reach for it (you should reach carefully and slowly, avoiding sudden, frightening gestures), then ask to see another. Ask the pet shop owner to place the hamster on a table so you can observe it better. The older a hamster is, the more set it will be in its ways. Therefore, one that is just matured, about five to eight weeks old, is best.

Unless you plan to breed them, you can purchase one hamster, because they don't mind being alone. What a hamster does mind, however, is being bored, and his cage will need an exercise wheel.

If you can get a treadmill and a ladder as well, so much the better. A bored hamster is not above pulling at its cage and scattering its litter or nesting material all over the place. Once your hamster has gotten to know you, daily exercise outside the cage will be helpful.

Hamsters need a cage that is large enough to provide separate areas for sleeping, eating, and eliminating. Because it is such an active little animal, about 1 square foot of cage per hamster is necessary. A metal hamster cage with a tray that slides out of the bottom to facilitate cleaning is best.

The bottom of the cage should be lined with a good absorbent material such as cedar shavings, cat litter, or paper toweling. The hamster will prefer the paper because it can be shredded, an activity hamsters savor.

You will need a gravity-flow bottle for water and a feeding dish that can be fastened securely to the inside of the cage, because a dish that rests on the bottom of the cage will soon be knocked over, scattering its contents, messing the cage, and wasting food.

Hamsters prefer to sleep in a box. It should be of metal and have a removable top for cleaning. If you do not give your hamster a box, it will build a nest of the absorbent material from the bottom of the cage. Like humans, hamsters need occasional privacy. It is best to keep its cage in a shaded place, away from direct sun. Hamsters are nocturnal, and once the sun has set, your pet will come out of its nest and start its activities.

The cage must be cleaned at least once a week. Unless you have been very sparing with food, you will find some stored away. It is advisable to restore as much of this food as possible to its original location after the cleaning. Otherwise, the hamster will search for it, and will become upset when unable to find its hoard. The same procedure applies to the bedding. Unless it is soiled, it should be removed intact for the cleaning, then replaced where it was found.

Generally, a hamster will urinate in the same location every day—at the side of the cage opposite its nest. Clean this area daily. If you do not, it will begin to smell.

The water bottle should be washed and the water changed daily. Hamsters eat typical rodent fare: nuts, grains, seeds, grasses, and some fruits and vegetables. Dry commercial hamster food is available and inexpensive, but supplement it with the other foods mentioned above. Give foods containing a high percentage of water, such as lettuce, sparingly. Because hamsters hoard, they will hide this food, and its water content will cause it to decay rapidly, promoting bacterial growth and odor.

It is fun to watch a hamster fill its pouches with food, and there is no need to worry about overeating with a hamster. It won't, no matter how much food is around.

Since hamsters are also gnawing animals, something hard, like nuts or a piece of hardwood, should be kept in the cage at all times.

Of all the rodent pets, hamsters are the most nervous. Therefore, until your hamster is at home in its cage, gloves should be used to handle it. Make no sudden moves; do nothing to startle the animal. Speak softly to it and be reassuring. After a few days, you can start training it. Hamsters love raisins, peanuts, and sunflower seeds. Tempt your pet by placing one or two of these items in the palm of your hand and putting it in the cage. It will soon come over and start to eat from your hand. After several days, carefully pick the hamster up by gripping it firmly around the body. Be gentle.

You can teach a hamster to stand on its hind legs and beg for food. Also, if you are patient and repeat its name every time you give it a favorite morsel of food, you can teach it to come when its name is called.

Once they are tame enough to let out of the cage, be very careful. A grown hamster can fit through an opening the size of a quarter and, once gone, is difficult to retrieve. A hamster will gnaw on wooden furniture and be delighted to make his bed from the tufting inside a favorite and expensive couch. Remember what happened to me when my pet hamsters escaped.

The female hamster has the shortest gestation period of any domesticated rodent, sixteen days. She can have her first litter at two months of age, and if planned parenthood is not enforced, one litter a month thereafter. Just think how many cages that would require at the end of a year, counting an average of seven babies to the litter each time. One hundred thousand would be a good approximation!

When breeding hamsters, never put the male into the female's cage. She is liable to attack him because it is an invasion of her territory. It is a good idea to place both cages side by side and give the pair a chance to get accustomed to each other. Then try putting the female into the male's cage. If she is ready to breed, she will raise her tail and lower her head. Both animals will then run around the cage until the female stops, ready to accept the male. If the female isn't ready, she will attack the male, so be prepared to separate the pair before they hurt each other.

Since hamsters are nocturnal and prefer to mate in the early evening, it is best to put them together after sunset. If the hamsters accept each other peacefully, it is all right to leave them together for about a week and then return the female to her own cage. Provide a nesting box with extra nesting material in the cage with which she can build her nest. About sixteen days after mating, her litter will be born. Don't clean the cage or handle the litter unless absolutely essential. A female will not hesitate to destroy one or all of her offspring if she is upset by your handling of the babies. They will be weaned in three weeks and should be separated by sex at that time to keep them from breeding too soon. To determine sex, hold the hamster up and look at its underbelly. The male will have a penis about ¼ inch from its vent. The female vulva is closer to the vent and is hairless.

Hamsters can and do catch cold. The most effective treatment is warmth and rest.

Hamsters can also be attacked by mites and lice. If this should happen, thoroughly clean and disinfect the cage. Whether the animal likes it or not, throw out all of its stored food and bedding material and treat the hamster with a commercial powder.

GUINEA PIGS

Guinea pigs are the largest of the popular domestic rodents. A full grown animal is about 10 inches long and weighs close to 3 pounds. For many years guinea pigs served as experimental laboratory animals, hence the term "human guinea pig" to describe someone who is being used for experimentation or research.

Guinea pigs are no longer used extensively for research because their rate of reproduction is low compared to other rodents. The gestation period for a sow (female guinea pig) is about ten weeks, and the litters are usually small, averaging three.

Guinea pigs do not come from Guinea, nor are they pigs. The guinea pig is a rodent, and because its scientific name is *Cavia cutleri,* it is commonly called cavy. No one knows for certain why cavies are called guinea pigs. What is known is that this animal was first domesticated by pre-Inca Indians in Peru about eight hundred years ago, and that they were imported into England from Guiana. Because they do grunt and squeal like pigs, it is likely that they were first referred to as Guiana pigs and that in time this usage was corrupted. That, however, is speculation.

There are many breeds of guinea pigs. The differences among them are principally in the length, color, and texture of their fur. The color ranges from solids, including black, white, brown, and beige to albinos, patterns, and two-tones. Some resemble the coloring of Siamese cats, having light-colored bodies and ears, feet, and snout of darker coloring. The fur can be short, long, or rough with fur that swirls.

A guinea pig. (*American Museum of Natural History*)

All guinea pigs are of similar shape and size, however. They are stubby, with short legs, blunt noses, and furless ears. Guinea pigs have no tail.

Housing requirements for guinea pigs are somewhat different than for other rodents. First, the animals need a larger space in which to live. They do not jump or climb, so no exercise wheel or other elaborate equipment is required. Guinea pigs prefer a sleeping box and thick bedding material to cover the floor of their home. Use wood shavings, sawdust, straw, or shredded paper. The cage should be kept in a warm location away from drafts. A temperature range of 60 to 90 degrees should be maintained.

During warm weather, guinea pigs can be kept outdoors in hutches, but care should be taken to keep them out of strong sun.

The cage you use to house your guinea pig should provide about 2 square feet per animal. For one cavy, a 12- by 24-inch floor space is required. A cage about 36 inches long by 24 inches wide will house up to three guinea pigs comfortably.

Guinea pigs are not difficult to feed, but they do have one special requirement: they cannot synthesize vitamin C, so it must be a part of their regular diet. Vegetables such as carrots and lettuce are good sources of vitamin C, but the surest method of getting vitamin C into your pet is in the form of guinea pig pellets, which many pet shops carry. Pelletized foods for rabbits or hamsters can also be used, but make certain they contain the essential vitamin.

Guinea pigs are vegetarians and will eat just about any vegetable. They also like grasses, some fruits, dandelion leaves, and grains, such as oats, dry corn, and barley meal. The cavy will eat whole-wheat bread and bran as well.

If guinea pigs are fed high water content vegetables, such as lettuce and tomatoes, they can do without water.

However, it is a good idea to keep a gravity-flow bottle in the cage just in case. In addition, guinea pigs should have salt available. It can be purchased in small blocks in pet shops.

Guinea pigs are cute but not brilliant. Consequently, the food supply should be kept off the floor of their cage, since they don't know enough not to soil it if it is left there. Use food cups and trays that can be mounted on the side of the cage.

The long-haired variety of guinea pig can be groomed like a dog or cat. You can use a soft hairbrush, or a toothbrush if you have one of the rough-haired varieties of cavy.

Guinea pigs sometimes need a bath. Use mild soap and lukewarm water and be careful not to get soap into its mouth, ears, eyes, or nose. It is best to give your pet a bath in the tub, making sure there are no more than two or three inches of water in the tub. Towel dry your cavy and keep it warm and out of drafts until it is thoroughly dry.

Breeding

Guinea pigs have a gestation period of about ten weeks, and their average litter is three, with one to six offspring per litter. A sow can have up to five litters a year, but that is pushing her.

Since guinea pigs reach puberty at the age of one month, it is a good idea to separate the sexes as soon as they are weaned, which is three weeks after birth.

Professional breeders place as many as six sows with one boar (male guinea pig). The pet owner need simply place one male with one female, and nature will surely take its course. To tell males and females apart, press down gently on either side of the body opening. If the animal is a male, a small penis will appear.

If your male and female do not appear to be romantically inclined after you have placed them together, don't worry. The female's estrous (mating) cycle is about seventeen days long. She will accept the advances of the male only on one or two days (usually the second) of the cycle. You will have to leave the pair together for two or three weeks to be sure a complete cycle has passed.

The young are born with a full coat of fur, with teeth, and with their eyes open. They will soon be running around and within three days will be capable of taking solid food, while continuing to nurse.

By the time they are weaned, the young will weigh about half a pound. They continue to grow for a year and a half.

Under good conditions, guinea pig females can produce offspring until they are about four or five years old. They can live to be seven years of age, sometimes a little more.

Although guinea pigs can be infected with a wide range of ailments under laboratory conditions, as pets they are generally disease-free if certain rules are followed.

Perhaps the most important rule is cleanliness. The cage should be cleaned thoroughly at least once a week but more often if required. It should also be kept dry.

If the animal should show signs of having fleas or ticks, a standard spray or powder should be used, and its housing cleaned thoroughly. If your pet should lose its appetite for several days and also develop a cough, runny nose, or other cold symptoms, immediately separate it from the other pigs, if there are others, and keep the animal warm. If symptoms persist, call your veterinarian.

RABBITS

Technically, rabbits are not rodents. But because they behave so much like rodents, we won't harp on the fact that they are lagomorphs, because that would be splitting hares!

Rabbits breed and eat at a furious pace, and many rural

and suburban homeowners consider them pests, particularly those people who are growing ornamental plants and shrubs or are trying to grow vegetables or flowers. If there are rabbits around, it is impossible to grow lettuce, dahlias, and a host of other plants, without a rabbit-proof fence.

For the pet owner, on the other hand, rabbits are wonderful creatures. They are very soft and gentle and have been developed in a wide range of colors, shapes, and varieties. They are quiet, yet very active.

If you are going to bring a rabbit into your home, make certain you have enough room. The hutch should be at least 3 feet long by 2 feet wide by 2 feet high.

Like rodents, rabbits are gnawing animals, and it is essential to keep a piece of hardwood in the hutch. Rabbits also need salt.

Pet shops that sell rabbits will also sell rabbit pellets. This food contains all the nutrients necessary to keep a healthy, happy rabbit, and breeders seldom feed their animals anything else. But your pet will be better off emotionally if you vary its diet with carrots, lettuce, or young dandelion leaves, which rabbits really relish. They like to munch on hay, and this should be made available regularly.

A white rabbit. (*American Museum of Natural History*)

Rabbits also love clover, spinach, beet tops, and turnips, as well as dahlia leaves and a whole host of other ornamental vegetation. It is advisable, however, to limit the intake of these items, for rabbits do not know when to stop eating, and unless they are rationed, your rabbit will become obese and sluggish.

In the wild, rabbits eat incessantly, but they are also constantly moving about. In contrast, your pet rabbit will probably get little exercise.

A dish of fresh water in the hutch at all times is essential.

There are many varities of rabbit available as pets. The most popular are the New Zealand whites, bicolored Dutch belted, and Angora. All are gentle and lovable.

Anyone playing with a rabbit should remember never to pick one up by its ears. A rabbit should be picked up by gripping the loose skin over its shoulders with one hand, while the other hand gently supports the body either under the rump or around the midsection.

Domesticated rabbits rarely bite, but it is a good idea to tame a new rabbit by stroking it gently and leaving it inside the hutch for several days before taking it out. It can then be handled and carried anywhere.

Rabbits are not ideal as indoor pets. They will be better off in an outdoor hutch, which should be of good size. The standard rabbit hutch is two-thirds screened play area and one-third closed-in sleeping or breeding area. The enclosed portion should be covered with wood or some opaque material such as canvas or burlap. Bedding material should also be provided. The best is hay, which the rabbit can also munch on. The hutch must be cleaned two or three times a week.

Much has been said about the rapidity with which rabbits breed. It is all true. The doe (female rabbit) is polyestrous, which means that she goes into heat just about every time she sees a male. Consequently, to breed rabbits all you have to do is put a male and female together, and a family is on the way.

It is best to put the female into the male's cage. After mating, the female is returned to her hutch. About a month afterward, she will begin to build a nest with the fresh straw or hay that you have put in her hutch. She will have her litter within a day or so of building her nest. She will be nervous at this time, so avoid disturbing her, if at all possible.

Baby rabbits are born without fur, and their eyes remain closed approximately ten days. Don't touch them during this time or the mother may kill them. Although a litter can have as many as fifteen to eighteen offspring, the average size is six.

By the time the babies are three weeks old, they will be hopping about the hutch and taking pellets. They are weaned at about six weeks and at six months are ready to raise families of their own.

A healthy rabbit can live as long as ten years. As with rodents, the key to good health is nourishing food and a clean hutch. It is also a good idea to keep them away from other animals.

Rabbits are subject to attack by fleas and mites; if this happens, the animal should be treated with a powder and the hutch should be thoroughly cleaned. Rabbits are also susceptible to colds and internal parasites. Symptoms to watch for, in addition to sniffles, are loss of appetite and prolonged diarrhea. A veterinarian should be consulted.

3

CATS

Although cats have been domesticated for more than four thousand years, they have changed very little in that time. Today there are two basic types—the long-haired Persians and the shorthairs, which include both domestic and foreign cats like the Abyssinian, Burmese, Manx, Russian Blue, and Siamese.

Domestic shorthairs are the most common cats seen in the United States. The familiar alley cat, which most city dwellers know so well, is a shorthair. Another shorthair is the Abyssinian, which probably originated in Europe rather than Africa as its name implies. The most striking feature of the Abyssinian is its range of colors, which include brick and copper tones. Abyssinians are gentle and loving and don't make much noise.

Siamese cats are the most exotic of the shorthairs. They come from Thailand, Burma, or India. They were introduced into England toward the end of the last century and became immediate favorites. They have long, tapered heads, deep blue eyes, and "points"; their extremities—paws, tail, ears, and face—are a deeper shade of their body coloring. Thus, a sealpoint has a light brown body with dark brown points.

A common domestic short-haired cat. (*Patricia F. Fishtein*)

Burmese shorthairs originated in Burma. Their head and eyes are more rounded than the Siamese, making them look less oriental than the latter. Most common colorings are blues and deep copper tones, with golden eyes.

The Manx cat is of special interest among the shorthairs because it is completely without a tail, not even a stump. The Manx is the worst-tempered of all cats raised as pets. This breed comes in many colors and has long legs; because Manx cats' hind legs are longer than their forelegs, they appear to be pitched at an angle when they walk.

Persians are the most regal and beautiful of all the cats. With their round heads, flattened faces, and long, lush, beautifully colored coats, they have the stately appearance of royalty. Persians are loving and affectionate, follow their owners around the house, and do not like to be left alone. They are cuddly and lovable and clearly the best cat to have as a pet, although owners of other cats would disagree.

Literally hundreds of books have been written about cats, and it would be foolhardy to pretend that we can hope to cover everything in the relatively few pages we have allocated to cats. Suffice to say that cat lovers may have to go to their library, bookshop, or pet store for more detailed information.

Before You Buy

Once you have decided to get a cat, there are some things you need to know. The cat you buy should be at least eight weeks old. Younger kittens are not ready to be taken from the mother. One method of determining whether a cat is ready for adoption is to check its mouth. It should have two rows of sharp white teeth.

Reba and Kala, the author's beautiful Persian cats. (*Steve Curreri***)**

Before you take the cat home, watch it carefully. Is it playful or listless? Does it walk well and are its legs steady? Is it bloated? Are its eyes clear? Does its spine protrude? Move your finger back and forth in front of its face. Do the eyes follow your finger as you move it? Clap your hands together briskly behind the cat. Does it react? If not, perhaps its hearing is impaired.

Does it scratch itself more than seems reasonable? This is a judgmental matter, but surely you have seen and watched cats and kittens before. Therefore, you should be able to tell whether your potential pet has lice, fleas, or ticks.

Most people get their cat from a friend, a humane society, a pet shop, or a breeder. If you get a cat from one of the latter two, chances are you will be buying a purebred animal and paying a lot of money for it. There are certain things you are entitled to. Be sure the animal has papers and has been registered with an accredited organization. Find out how to have the ownership papers changed. If the cat hasn't been registered, ask the seller to tell you how to do it.

What Kind to Get

If you are planning to breed cats, you will want a female, because they produce the litters, and there is usually little profit to be made from breeding a male. In addition, males that have not been neutered are messy to have around. They often urinate on various objects to demonstrate their virility and territorial rights, and the odor they leave is unpleasant. So if you choose a male cat, have him neutered unless you are planning to breed him.

Actually, the same applies to females. Unless you want to raise one or more litters, it is advisable to have a female cat spayed. A female in heat will be very noisy and unhappy for about ten days and quite a nuisance to yourself and the neighbors. If she gets out and a male gets to her, there is the problem of disposing of the litter later on.

As far as temperaments are concerned, it doesn't depend on the cat's sex as much as it does on the individual animal. Cats are more aloof than dogs and less affectionate, but in their own quiet way, most cats—even those with a reputation for being standoffish—can be very loving and gregarious.

Feeding

Cats are nibblers. They rarely will empty a whole dish of food. Rather, they will take a few bites and go on to other business. This presents a problem. Moist cat food has a tendency to become stale rapidly, so it is never a good idea to fill your cat's bowl very full. It is better to put in a little food at a time so that you will have less to throw away.

Supermarket shelves are filled to the brim with cat foods, and what you feed your pet will depend upon its preference. When you first obtain your pet, it is a good idea to find out what it has been eating and stick pretty much to that diet for a while. Cats are carnivorous, and their staple food will consist of meats and fish. But most cats will also eat table scraps, including eggs and some vegetables. It is also advisable to supplement their diet with dry food pellets.

As just about everyone knows, cats love milk, and kittens should have it daily to promote good bone formation. Adult cats, however, do not need milk on a regular basis, because too much can upset their stomachs. Fresh water is a must. Change the water in the bowl at least once a day and keep both water and food dishes clean. Even in immaculate homes, food left standing tends to attract flies and insects.

Housebreaking

One reason for the great popularity of cats is that they are very clean animals and can be housebroken almost automatically. All you need is a litter box which is easily accessible to the cat and some litter. There are various brands of cat litter available in supermarkets and pet stores. Litter absorbs moisture and odors. A new cat should be shown where its litter box is, and you should gently rub its paws in the litter. If the cat makes a mistake and goes outside the litter box, place its waste in the box and put the cat in it. Your pet will soon learn. Solid material should be removed daily and flushed down the toilet. Moisture should be covered with fresh litter and the litter stirred. The contents of the litter box should be replaced at least once a week and the box cleaned thoroughly.

Bedding

Cats are rarely caged. Those that are will be miserable. Plan on giving your cat the run of the house. It will need a warm, cozy place to sleep. There are numerous cat beds and different types of bedding available, but it is most likely that your cat will prefer to sleep in your bed. If you find this a bother, set up a bed in your bedroom for it. When the cat jumps into your bed, tell it "no" firmly and squeeze its paws gently, but hard enough to let it feel the pressure as you put it back on the floor. It will soon learn to stay off the bed.

A scratching post is another necessity for a cat. This can be purchased in a pet shop, or you can try a piece of log about a foot long. Once the cat discovers its post, hopefully it will spend hours scratching it instead of the furniture.

Brushing and Grooming

Cats groom themselves constantly and rarely need bathing. But bathing sometimes becomes necessary, especially with long-haired varieties. Use lukewarm water and a mild soap. Be careful not to get soap in its eyes. Do it as quickly as possible, dry the cat thoroughly, and keep it out of drafts for a while.

Short-haired cats rarely need brushing. With longhairs, brushing is an absolute must, both from the standpoint of cosmetics and to remove loose hair. All cats preen themselves often and tend to accumulate hairs in their stomach. These fur balls can cause vomiting. This is nothing serious. Give your cat a few drops of mineral oil or cod liver oil and the problem should soon disappear. If there is frequent and persistent vomiting, diarrhea, or loss of appetite, a veterinarian should be consulted.

General Health

Cats are hardy, but like all living creatures, they become ill periodically. The most common ailments are vomiting, diarrhea, and constipation. These symptoms are usually related to diet or the formation of fur balls. For diarrhea, change the diet. Add more bulk, such as pellets. If you have been giving your cat milk, stop for a while. If the problem does not clear up in a few days, call a vet.

Cats are subject to a virulent disease called feline enteritis, or cat distemper. They can be inoculated against this sometimes fatal disease. You should not purchase a cat unless you know it has been inoculated, or unless you plan to have your veterinarian do it. Kittens receive two shots, with a booster given to the adult several years later.

Cats are susceptible to bronchitis. The symptoms are hacking cough and difficulty in breathing. Keep the animal warm, and if you have a vaporizer, use it to moisten the air. Hold the cat very gently but firmly and take its temperature rectally. If it is over 102 degrees and remains that way for a day, call your vet.

Cats also can get several kinds of worms, such as tapeworm, hookworm, and roundworm. Your vet will require a stool sample to analyze in order to determine the proper treatment. Symptoms of worms are loss of appetite, an itching and inflamed anus, and general lethargy.

Breeding

Although female cats go into their first heat when they are about six months old, it is not advisable to breed them until they are a year old. Once they start, most cats come into heat in the spring and again in the fall. It lasts about two weeks.

About one week after the female goes into heat, she will be ready to accept a male. If you intend to breed your cat, you will probably purchase a pedigreed cat and will want a tom of the same strain but different lineage. It is advisable to contact a breeder and make arrangements to bring your female to the male for several days.

The gestation period of cats is eight to nine weeks.

About five weeks into her pregnancy, give the cat milk every day and increase the amount of solid food in her diet.

A nest box should be provided, with sides about six or eight inches high to prevent the kittens from crawling out. Put plenty of papers down under the box and place several layers of old towels inside the box. These can be removed and washed or discarded after the kittens are born.

It takes an average of four to six hours for a litter to be born. There may be anywhere from one to eight kittens. If your cat seems to be laboring too long, call the vet and speak to him or her about it.

After the kittens are born, keep feeding the mother

extra milk and food. She needs it to take care of the family. Food, water, and the litter box should be kept close to the nest. As soon as the kittens are able to move around, their mother will train them to the litter box. They are born deaf and blind, but in about ten days their eyes will open, and after five weeks they will start supplementing their diet of mother's milk with solid foods. Kitten foods are available in pet shops and supermarkets, but it is a good idea to speak to your vet about special foods as well. You can feed kittens strained baby foods if you like—beef, fish, liver, or egg yolk.

By the time they are two months old the kittens will be completely weaned, at which time they should be taken to the veterinarian for their inoculations.

A Word of Warning

One problem you may run into with cats concerns plants. Some cats are obsessively drawn to houseplants. They may play with them, tear at them, or eat them. Since many plants brought into the home can be poisonous to cats, it is absolutely essential to know whether any varieties you have are toxic. Hang or place those which are toxic where they are inaccessible to your cat. Philodendron and dieffenbachia are just two of the common houseplants that are dangerous. Your veterinarian may know whether any of the plants you have pose these dangers, or you may ask your county agricultural agent or an official of a botanical garden.

In addition, some outdoor plants such as azaleas, English ivy, foxglove, and delphinium are very harmful, and your cat should be kept away from them.

4

BIRDS

GENERAL INFORMATION

Starting in about 1970, rigorous import restrictions on exotic birds such as mynahs, cockatiels, and some varieties of parrot made the cost of purchasing these birds prohibitive. The restrictions were imposed because of both humanitarian considerations—the birds were mistreated, and tens of thousands died before they reached the shores of the United States—and the fear of disease. Many of the imported birds carried a pneumonialike disease which could be transmitted to humans. Concern that birds would cause illness in humans affected the sales of those birds that pose no threat to health and can be bred easily in captivity—the canaries, finches, and parakeets.

Recently, however, with stringent health regulations proving effective, there has been an upsurge in the popularity of birds as pets. This renewed interest is well deserved. Birds are beautiful and a joy to have around the house. Some sing, some can be taught to talk, and others can be trained to do tricks. Many become loving, devoted companions.

Whichever bird you decide upon for your pet, be certain it is in good condition. It should pass several simple tests. Its feathers should be sleek and neat, its eyes should be bright and clear, and the bird should be active and alert. If it is puffed up, that is a sign of possible trouble. As is the case with any pet, before you buy, observe and inspect. Whether you are buying from a pet shop, a breeder, or accepting it from a friend, don't be hasty.

HOUSING

All pet birds should be kept in cages, which can be purchased in a wide variety of sizes, shapes, and colors. The type you purchase will depend on personal preference, the amount of money you wish to spend, and the kind of bird you are buying. Small cages for a single canary are available at modest cost, but the larger the cage the better. It is unfair to confine in a tiny cage a creature whose natural inclination is to fly. If possible, your cage should be large enough to allow the bird to move about with some degree of freedom. It should have at least two per-

A suitable bird cage has two perches, a swing, and a tray that can be slid out for easy cleaning.

ches and a birdbath. Ladders, bells, chains, and swings should be provided to keep your pet from becoming bored. There should be at least one seed cup, one cup for water, and a cup for special treats.

FOOD

Birds cannot digest food without gravel, and this should be made available on the floor of the cage. Birds also need cuttlebone for calcium and for keeping their beaks trim.

It is preferable to have a cage with a removable bottom tray, so that you can clean it regularly without disturbing your bird too often. The birds described here are primarily seed eaters, and most pet shops carry a complete line of bird foods. Commercial mixes are available for all the birds described in this book. In addition, most birds love fruit and some vegetables, and their diet should be supplemented with these. A small piece of lettuce or apple, cherries, bananas, celery, and carrots are also favorites of most pet birds.

Fruits and vegetables should be fresh and crisp and should be removed from the cage as soon as they begin to wilt or discolor. Remember the expression, "to eat like a bird" when feeding your pet special treats. Birds do not eat very much, and giving them more than they can take is wasteful.

Remember that too much of a good thing or a sudden change in diet can give a bird diarrhea. Droppings should be firm and look like a bull's-eye, with a dark center and white exterior. If droppings become loose and watery, it is time either to change the diet or to watch your bird carefully because it may be getting sick. Chances are it's the diet.

GENERAL CARE

Once your bird gets to know you and feels comfortable in the house, it should be given exercise. This can become a regular routine when you clean the cage. Let the bird fly around the house. Just make certain the burners on the stove are off, and that all windows are closed. Other potential danger spots should be checked as well. There should be no hot water running anywhere, for example, and if there is a cat in the house it must be kept away. Unscreened fireplaces are a hazard too.

Birds such as parakeets can easily be finger-trained, and it should not be difficult to return a bird to its cage after it has had its fly about the house and you have thoroughly cleaned its cage. The well-being of most birds depends, among other things, on cleanliness, and the more immaculate a cage is the better off your bird will be. You will have to be the judge of how often to clean the cage, but the absolute minimum for any bird is once a week. All toys, perches, food, water cups, mirrors, bells, etc. should be cleaned and scrubbed.

Place the cage out of direct sunlight and out of the way of drafts. The temperature in the room should always be at least 70 degrees, although some birds can be happy at lower temperatures. If the room in which you keep your bird is drafty, the cage can be covered with a piece of clear plastic.

Some birds, such as parakeets, canaries, and finches, can be bred easily in captivity. Details will be given.

CANARIES

Singing canaries are among the most delightful of the cage birds. Canary enthusiasts have gone to great lengths to train their birds to sing on cue and enter the birds in competitions all over the country.

A singing canary. (*Patricia F. Fishtein*)

Singing canaries are classified as either choppers, or rollers or warblers—the first uttering a type of staccato chirping, and the others producing a more continuous and varied song. A good singing canary is a great delight to have around the house.

Generally speaking, only the males sing. Whether you purchase your bird from a breeder or a pet shop, be certain to get a written guarantee that the bird you purchase will sing. But don't expect a canary to start singing the moment you get him into the house. He has, after all, been through a traumatic experience. He has been taken from his friends, put into a dark cardboard box, transported roughly for a while, and then been thrust into an entirely new environment. Would you want to sing after such an ordeal?

Once your bird is in his cage, try to keep away from him as much as possible. Let him get accustomed to his new quarters. Give him about a week to ten days. By then, he should start singing. If he doesn't, it is likely that your he is a she.

Varieties

Type-canaries are raised primarily for their color, although size and shape are also taken into consideration when they are judged. The following are some of the more popular of the type-canaries.

Red Factors range in color from reddish-orange through various coppertones, to orange and yellow-orange. They are quite spectacular. As an added bonus, these beautifully colored birds can also sing. Red factors are a product of cross-breeding between canaries and the South American red finch, with whom canaries were found to be compatible.

Lizard, or *Frosted,* canaries are deeper colored, with white feather tips.

Other popular types are *Yorkshires,* which can grow up to 10 inches in length, and the *Norwich,* which frequently has crested, or tufted, head feathers.

Molting

All birds go through periods when they lose feathers. Canaries molt either in the spring or in late summer. During this time they are most fragile and susceptible to disease. Canaries generally don't breed during their molting season.

Feeding

There are an ample number of canary food mixes on the market. These generally consist of an assortment of small seeds, including rape and millet.

In addition, song food, conditioning food, and molting foods provide supplementary proteins, vitamins, and minerals for your bird. Canaries are also fond of egg biscuits. Generally, all needed food supplements can be obtained in the various treat foods available for canaries in pet shops.

Ailments

Canaries are subject to respiratory diseases such as colds, asthmatic attacks, and even pneumonia. The primary treatment is warmth. If possible, the temperature should be raised to about 85 degrees. This can be done by mounting incandescent bulbs close to the cage and leaving them on day and night. Be sure to keep a thermometer nearby and make certain the cage doesn't overheat. Do not permit the temperature to go above 90 degrees. Symptoms of a respiratory ailment are puffiness, heavy breathing, sneezing, and perhaps wheezing. Medicines are available in pet stores. These can be added to the food or the water supply. If your bird remains on the floor of the cage, move food and water down there. Remember, the best treatment is prevention. A clean cage and a draft-free location are essential.

Mites or Lice

To treat birds for mites or lice, use one of the many powders available in pet stores. Treat not only the bird, but the cage too. Follow the instructions on the powder label. Symptoms are signs of discomfort such as itching, rubbing against the cage, and loss of feathers.

Breeding

Breeding canaries, like breeding other living creatures, can be educational, fun, and profitable, too. You will need time, patience, and, of course, a male and a female.

You may have to rely on the breeder or pet shop proprietor to provide you with a pair. Differentiating between the sexes is difficult. As indicated before, the male usually sings. Females chirp. That's no guarantee, but it is a fairly reliable method of telling them apart.

Canaries are generally bred in late winter and early spring, when the days grow noticeably longer and the sun is higher in the sky.

You will need a breeding cage and a nest. A breeding cage is a special cage, about twice as long as it is wide, with two partitions in the center, a wire one and a solid one. Nests can be purchased at most pet shops, or you can make one by using a metal strainer about four inches in diameter, removing the handle, and fastening it on the inside of the cage, midway between the top and floor of the cage.

With both partitions in place, the female is placed in the section containing the nest and the male is placed in the other one. Once the birds are accustomed to their new environment, remove the solid partition, allowing them to get a look at each other. Their mating call sounds like a shrill whistle. When you hear it, it is time to remove the wire partition. Place small pieces of string, cotton, grass cuttings, wool, and any other small, soft materials in the cage. Canaries lay from three to four eggs, one every other day. They will begin to hatch in fourteen to fifteen days.

It is a good idea to remove the male to a nearby cage once the eggs are laid. Although there are differences of opinion, the consensus is that the male doesn't contribute significantly to the raising of the young, and more often than not he will bother the female. Furthermore, if placed in a nearby cage, he is likely to start singing.

The mother will feed her young and take care of them until they are ready for weaning. That will take about six weeks. You must be sure to have plenty of treat food, egg biscuit, and standard canary food available at all times. In addition, more frequent feedings of special fruit and vegetable treats, such as apple and lettuce should be given.

FINCHES

Finches are among the most versatile of cage birds. There are literally hundreds of different varieties, ranging in size from a few inches to over a foot long. They are available in many different colors and color combinations and are native to just about every part of the world. The cost of a pair of finches will vary from inexpensive to extremely expensive, depending on the type. For the beginner, the society and zebra finches are the most popular.

These small birds are beautiful, active, moderately priced, and easy to obtain in most pet shops. They are 3 to 4½ inches long, have small beaks, and live principally on small seeds, fruits, and vegetables.

Most pet shops sell finch food, which is generally made up of different types of millet seed. Finches will not touch rape seed, one of the staples of canary mixes. It is therefore not advisable to feed finches with canary mixes. It is always a good idea to vary the diet of your bird. Try apple, orange, berries, lettuce, or celery. Like canaries, finches need gravel or grits, cuttlebone, and treat foods.

Ailments

Finches are susceptible to the same ailments as canaries and the same parasites that attack canaries also attack finches. See the section on canary ailments for symptoms and treatment.

Cages

Finches are more active than canaries—they fly faster and are more nervous. Therefore, they need more room. They are also social birds and do best when kept together with at least one more of their species. It is therefore advisable to have as large a cage as possible, no smaller than 24 inches long and at least 12 to 15 inches in width and height.

Breeding

If you wish to breed finches, the easiest of all are the zebras. Unlike some species, zebras are easy to tell apart. The males have red beaks and distinctive reddish brown markings on their cheeks and flanks.

Finches like closed nest boxes. You can use commercially available finch nests, or you can make your own, using a piece of hollowed out tree limb, a dried gourd, or an enclosed wooden bird's nest with a 1 inch opening (available in most pet shops).

Nesting materials can include small pieces of yarn, rope, wool, cotton, or grass clippings.

The eggs hatch in about two weeks from the time they are laid. You can expect from two to four eggs, and the babies can fend for themselves in about five weeks.

PARAKEETS

Parakeets are the most popular of all cage birds. They are brilliantly colored. They are active and amusing, they can be finger-trained easily, and most can be taught to talk. Parakeets are loving, bright, and highly entertaining. It's no wonder they are so popular.

Parakeets are small birds, about 7½ inches long and weighing 1½ to 2 ounces, and they look like small parrots. As a matter of fact, the word parakeet stems from the French *perroquet,* meaning "little parrot." Once the bird was imported into America, *perroquet* quickly became parakeet.

Although various species of parakeet are found in many parts of the world, it is the Australian parakeet that is outstanding in terms of its versatility as a pet. The aborigines of Australia call this amusing bird, *betcherrygah,* meaning "pretty bird." In time, the Australian word was anglicized and became budgerigar—budgie, for short. Now, the terms parakeet and budgie are used interchangeably.

The original parakeets that were exported from Australia were found only in varying shades of green. They were easy to breed in captivity, however, and before long breeders had developed blue, yellow, and white budgies.

Distinguishing the sex of adult parakeets is generally quite easy. All parakeets have a layer of thick skin on the upper part of the beak. This layer of skin, called the cere, is deep blue in mature males, and pink, tan, or pale blue in females.

In choosing your bird, make sure its eyes are clear and that it is active. Do not pick a bird that just sits on its perch and is all puffed out. As in the case of all cage birds, give your parakeet plenty of room and, if you can, lots of toys to play with. Parakeets love to amuse themselves with bells and mirrors and on ladders and swings.

The essential cage furnishings consist of a seed cup and a water cup. There should also be at least one treat cup. The bird will thoroughly enjoy a birdbath—once it's accustomed to it—but it's not absolutely necessary.

Ample supplies of parakeet seed are found in most pet shops. That is the budgie's staple food. There should also be a supply of regular treat foods to supplement its diet with vitamins and minerals. Most parakeets have one provoking habit. When they eat, they have a tendency to dehusk their seeds, then swallow the seed and return the empty husk to the seed cup. This frequently makes it appear that the cup is full of food when, in fact, it's full of empty husks. Check the food cup carefully every day, since budgies get very cross when hungry.

Gravel on the floor of the cage is essential because it helps your bird digest its food.

Parakeets can learn to eat and enjoy a wide range of foods people eat. Many trained parakeets have been known to sit at the table with a family, usually on a favorite person's shoulder, and share many a delicacy with them. Don't overdo it, though.

It is a good idea to feed your parakeet a small quantity of greens regularly. Fruits are also welcome, but diarrhea isn't, so take it easy when introducing new foods to your bird's diet.

A parakeet, the most popular of all cage birds. (*Patricia F. Fishtein*)

Training

Parakeets are basically very friendly birds. They can be finger-trained easily, taught to do tricks, and, if you are patient, will even learn to talk. But before you attempt to teach your pet anything, you must gain its confidence.

First, it is a good idea to give your parakeet a few days to get accustomed to its new home. Make sure it has plenty of food and water (which should be changed every day), and do not startle it with any loud noises or abrupt moves. Speak to it softly and gently when you are near the cage, but don't make a nuisance of yourself.

After a few days, slip a smooth stick or perch through the cage and bring it slowly toward your pet. Speak softly and reassuringly as you do so. Press the perch very gently against its abdomen. Perhaps it won't happen with the first try, but in a relatively short time the parakeet will step up onto the perch. Repeat this a number of times. When the bird is accustomed to this procedure, substitute your finger for the perch. It will be necessary for you to open the door of the cage and put your hand in. Remember to move very slowly and speak very reassuringly.

It is a good idea after each successful training session to reward your bird with something special, such as a piece of lettuce or apple, so that your budgie associates stepping onto your finger with something pleasant. As these steps are repeated, your bird will become more and more secure. Before long it will realize that it has found a new friend.

The next step in the training process is to take the bird out of the cage on your finger. Unscreened doors and windows should be closed when you do this. If the bird will be flying around the kitchen, make sure nothing hot is around.

Chances are your bird's first experience flying outside the cage will be trying for both of you. It is probably the first time your bird has ever been outside a cage, and the experience is apt to be a little frightening. Be reassuring. Don't panic. When it is time to return the bird to the cage, try to take the bird in your hand, on your finger, or on the training perch. The basic rule is make no abrupt movements or loud noises.

It should not be difficult to return your bird to its cage because flying around the house will be very tiring for it. In time, your bird will probably learn to return to its cage when it is ready to do so. To encourage this, it is a good idea to buy a landing perch to place outside the cage door.

Most bird books don't mention this, but you will undoubtedly have a bit of cleaning up to do around the house after your bird has returned to its cage. Bird droppings are fairly easy to scoop up in a little plastic spoon, and any residue can easily be taken care of with mild soap and lukewarm water.

Parakeets will teach themselves to walk up and down a

ladder and to ring a bell. Some budgies will also learn to push a ball around.

Talking

Most parakeets can learn to talk. Repetition and patience are the keys. Pick out one word—the bird's name, your name, or hello, for instance, and get close to your bird and keep repeating the word. Don't make the lesson too long. It is better to have several short lessons throughout a day than one long one. The best time for a lesson is at night. Cover the cage so the bird has minimum distractions and gently repeat the word over and over.

Once your budgie has learned one word, you can start on another. He can acquire a fairly large vocabulary if you have the time, energy, and motivation.

Teaching your bird to talk will be easier if there are no other birds around. A parakeet's attention span is short to begin with; if there is another bird in the cage, it is infinitesimal.

The time it takes for your bird to learn to talk will vary. It may be as short as a month or as long as a year. If you are going to undertake such a project, it is best to start with a young bird. Three months old is the optimal age. Up to six or nine months is acceptable. The older a bird is, the more difficult it will be to teach it to talk.

If you don't have a great deal of time to spend yourself, you can buy training records in many pet shops. These are made by experts, and they work quite well.

Breeding

Breeding parakeets is easy, fun, and potentially profitable. All you need, besides a male and a female, is a relatively large cage and a nesting box. A commercial nesting box, for sale in some pet stores, consists of a wooden box about 10 inches long and about 6 inches high and wide. At one end is a hole about 1½ inches in diameter, in which a perch has been inserted. Within the nest is a block of wood about five inches square with a slight concave depression in it, having a maximum depth, at the center, of about half an inch. This is where the eggs will be laid and hatched. No nesting materials are needed. In their native Australia, parakeets nest in tree hollows, and their eggs are laid and hatched on wood.

Parakeet nests usually come equipped with a sliding wood partition, which can be lifted for a look at your pets' handiwork. Once you see your budgies making frequent trips to the nest, it is a good bet there are eggs inside. It will be about three weeks before all the eggs have hatched. If there are unhatched eggs, wait another week before removing them. If they haven't hatched by then, they aren't going to.

The young birds are born completely without feathers and will remain bare for about a week, after which fuzz starts to appear. The parents take care of all feeding until the young are weaned, in about five weeks. Just keep the parents well fed, with plenty of treats, condition food, and their favorite fruits and vegetables. Don't overfeed them, because if you do, they will get diarrhea.

A mated pair of parakeets will continue having offspring regularly, but it is best to limit their output to about two or three sets of young per year.

Problems

All birds molt; that is, they drop mature feathers and replace them with new young feathers. This can happen at any time, so don't worry. What isn't a normal molt is the appearance of bald spots on the bird, or loss of the ability to fly. This is most likely the result of some parasite, like mites or fleas, and the bird should be treated for this.

Parakeets, like other cage birds, are subject to colds and

pneumonia. The symptoms are wheezing, sneezing, and general discomfort. The bird will puff up, its eyes will be half-closed, and it will be listless and lack energy. Try to keep it well fed with its favorite foods if it will eat, and keep it warm, using a light bulb if necessary, to keep the cage at a temperature close to 85 degrees.

PARROTS

There are more than three hundred varieties of parrot to be found throughout the world's tropical and subtropical zones. Many are very beautiful, striking birds, and a few are among the most spectacular of cage birds. They are intelligent and affectionate, and some can become very good talkers.

A combination of strict import regulations and the inability of breeders to get some species to reproduce readily in captivity has cut the supply of the more exotic cage birds in this family severely. Those that are obtainable are often very expensive.

Nevertheless, several members of the parrot family are readily obtainable. These make good pets. They are fun to have around and are easy to keep. The following are among the most popular parrot types.

There are four species of *lovebird* available in pet stores. They are similar to budgies but not as friendly. Kept singly or in pairs, however, they can become good pets. They can be trained to do tricks and can be bred like parakeets. Mating them, however, is generally much more difficult than with budgies. If you want to breed them, your best bet is to purchase a pair from a breeder.

Bee Bee Parrots are small short-tailed birds comparable in size to lovebirds, rarely growing longer than 6 or 7 inches. The canary-winged bee bee is the most popular variety of parrot. These birds are responsive to attention and, after their initial timidity has worn off, enjoy being handled. They can be taught to talk and do the same tricks as parakeets.

Cockatiels are spectacular birds. They are relatively large, averaging about 12 inches in length, and are distinguished by a magnificent crest. They are easy to mate because most males have an identifiable orange spot on the cheek and females generally do not. They can be bred in captivity, but they need very large quarters. The breeding box alone should be at least 6 inches longer than the birds and should be about a foot square. Cockatiels eat the same foods as other parrots and parakeets. Because they are larger, they will also take peanuts, sunflower seeds, and grapes.

General Care of Parrots

All the rules that applied to canaries, finches, and parakeets apply to parrots. Clean the cage regularly and freshen the food and water daily.

The more toys you have for parrots, the less likely they are to become bored and the happier they will be. A bored parrot may tear out some of its feathers. If you are going to commit yourself to keeping a parrot, plan to give it plenty of attention.

Diseases are less likely to be a problem if you keep your bird clean, well fed, and out of drafts. Treatment, if necessary, is the same as for canaries.

One last word about parrots in general. Even tame parrots can be frightened easily by quick gestures and loud noises. Parrots have strong beaks and use them for self-defense. A frightened parrot, no matter how friendly at other times, is apt to bite. The larger the bird, the harder it bites. Painful bites are infrequent, but they do occur. If you have a parrot, always handle it with extreme care, particularly if it is a larger one.

MYNAH BIRDS

Mynahs are far and away the best talkers of all cage birds. In addition, they are great mimics. Not only do they imitate the human voice, but they imitate sounds as well. A close friend had a mynah that learned entire phrases, such as "How now brown . . . (it could never remember "cow") and "Birds can't talk." In addition, the bird imitated a squeaking door, a whistle, and a Santa Claus laugh. It was a great pet to have around, always a conversation piece.

Unfortunately, mynahs are not easily bred in captivity. This fact, coupled with import restrictions and the fact that they are native to Southeast Asia, make mynahs difficult to obtain and expensive when they are available.

In general, the mynahs are brought into the country during the late spring and summer.

These birds can be finger-trained and they will learn to perch on your head or shoulder. But they have so much

A mynah bird, the best talker of all cage birds. (*American Museum of Natural History*)

personality that it will not be necessary to teach your mynah many tricks in order for it to be entertaining.

Unlike the birds discussed thus far, mynahs are soft-billed and cannot eat seeds. They are partial to fruits, vegetables, and insects. The latter are not necessary, however, and your mynah will be perfectly content to live on a vegetarian diet, including the mynah pellets stocked by many pet shops.

Mynahs are larger than most cage birds, sometimes growing to a length of 10 inches. Consequently, they need a cage about 2 feet square with at least two perches, a large birdbath, and either a paper bag or cardboard box into which the bird can retreat when it wants privacy. At night the cage should be covered to give your pet additional privacy.

There are no special rules for caring for mynahs. A clean cage is essential and it should be kept in a draft-free location at a temperature of 65 degrees or higher.

Because mynahs are expensive, any illness should be discussed with a veterinarian promptly.

PIGEONS

Since this book is about house pets, we mention pigeons only in passing because most pigeons are raised and kept in coops outside the home. Pigeon-keeping is an interesting hobby, and enthusiasts raise pigeons for show, racing, homing, and, in some cases, because their owner enjoys watching his or her flock fly in circles above the rooftop.

Many books have been written about pigeon-keeping. Readers who have space on their rooftop or room on their property to set up a coop should look at one or more of these books. They are available in most libraries, bookstores, or pet shops.

5

REPTILES AND AMPHIBIANS

GENERAL INFORMATION

Reptiles and amphibians are discussed in one chapter because they have a number of physiological similarities. All reptiles and amphibians are cold-blooded, which means that they depend on their environment for body heat. That is why you will frequently see a frog or a snake, a lizard or a turtle, basking in the sun in an apparent daze. Both reptiles and amphibians are vertebrates; that is, they have a backbone.

There are also differences between reptiles and amphibians. Reptiles prefer higher temperatures, the range between 80 and 85 degrees being optimal. Amphibians like it cooler, 65 to 75 degrees is best for them. If the temperature of their environment drops below these levels, they become inactive and stop eating.

Amphibians are intermediate between fish and reptiles. Fish have gills and breathe in water. Reptiles—snakes, lizards, and turtles—breath air. Amphibians, such as frogs, toads, and newts, have gills in the larval state and

69

breathe in water, but as adults, they breath air, although they can spend considerable time underwater.

Reptiles generally have no legs and move on their bellies, like snakes, or have relatively short legs, like most types of lizards and turtles.

Not everyone takes readily to reptiles and amphibians. Unfortunately, this is a matter of conditioning. The thought of a snake can send shivers through almost everyone, and the words *slimy* and *poisonous* are often associated with the word *snake*. That is a misconception. Most snakes are neither poisonous nor slimy. They are gentle and relatively easy to keep as pets if a few basic requirements are met. Temperature is one requirement already mentioned. Another is food.

Most reptiles and amphibians require live food. Depending on the reptile's size, this can range from small worms to fish, mice, and rats. Not everyone enjoys watching a snake swallow a goldfish whole. Fewer still get a thrill from watching a mouse or a rat being devoured. In some cases, it is possible for a reptile or an amphibian to be tricked into eating ground meat instead of live food. This procedure is risky, however, and you may soon wind up with a dead pet if you are wedded to the concept of getting your pet to think it is eating live food when it isn't.

Since you will want to observe your pet, a glass aquarium is the preferred method of housing reptiles and amphibians. It is essential that a secure but removable top be used, to enable you to clean up regularly.

You will also need a heater for your pet. A bulb or an incandescent light that can be hung inside the tank will do. A thermometer is another essential piece of equipment. One of the principal reasons for failure with reptiles or amphibians as pets is a temperature which is either too low or too high for them.

Whether your pet is a reptile or an amphibian, water will have to be available.

Paper is the best material for lining the bottom of the aquarium, which should be fitted with rocks, twigs, or branches to make the environment as interesting and natural as possible.

If you are a beginner, your reptile or amphibian should be acquired only from a pet shop. If you live in the country, it is very tempting to try to capture a snake, lizard, or turtle from a local stream or pond. But since some snakes are poisonous and some turtles bite very hard, it is preferable to leave these animals in the wild alone.

Nearly every pet shop carries some kind of reptile or amphibian, whether a snake, lizard, turtle, toad, frog, newt, or chameleon. Some turtles are no longer available legally, although they were sold in pet shops by the millions as recently as five years ago. These animals were abused in many ways and died literally by the millions. To complicate the problem further, many turtles were responsible for spreading salmonellosis, an intestinal infection, among pet owners, especially children. As a result, the sale of turtles was severly restricted.

SNAKES

Snakes make very interesting pets. They are not much trouble to keep, they are neither noisy nor dirty, and they can be fascinating to watch, especially when they eat or shed their skin.

Perhaps the first thought that comes to mind when the word snake is mentioned is that they're poisonous. Actually, of the more than one hundred species native to the United States and Canada, only four are poisonous. These are the rattlesnake, the copperhead, the coral snake, and the water moccasin. Obviously, these cannot be kept as pets.

The most popular pet snakes are garter snakes, king snakes, and corn snakes. The only way to get a pet snake is through a reputable pet shop. Make certain its pet shop surroundings are clean. Its eyes should not be clouded over, and its body should be free of any kind of wound.

Feeding

Snakes are carnivorous and require live food. If you do not have the stomach to feed your pet snake a mouse, rat, frog, or fish twice a week, then snake-keeping is probably not for you.

Of the three kinds of snake that are most popular, king snakes and corn snakes prefer to eat animals (mice, rats, birds, frogs) they kill by constriction. The smaller garter snake likes fish, but will eat earthworms, as well. Garter snakes overpower their prey, take it into their mouths, and swallow it whole. Local pet shops sell goldfish, and since a small garter snake eats about two goldfish a week, it is not an expensive pet to keep. During the warm months, earthworms make a nice change in diet for your snake. These, too, are relatively inexpensive. If you have access to a place where you can dig your own, so much the better.

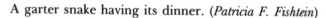

A garter snake having its dinner. (*Patricia F. Fishtein*)

Snakes that eat larger animals (mice, frogs, or smaller snakes) pose more of a problem. First, you will have to locate a source of this live food for these types of snakes. Secondly, sometimes your snake will not take readily to the food you offer, and it may be necessary to give it a hamster.

Housing

The best type of housing for a snake is a fish tank. The glass sides enable you to observe the snake, and a tank is easy to keep clean. It should be at least as long as the snake's body and half as wide and high. A 12-inch snake, for example, requires a 12-by 6-by 6-inch aquarium as a minimum. Since your snake is expected to grow, however, a larger size is desirable.

You will need a tight-fitting mesh top to cover the aquarium and prevent your pet from getting out. An inside light is also a necessity, both for illumination and heat. Snakes prefer a temperature between 80 and 85 degrees, but under no circumstances, should the temperature be allowed to fall below 75 degrees. Snakes begin to get sluggish at lower temperatures, and if they are in a state of semiconsciousness, they won't eat and won't be much fun to watch, either.

Furnishings for your aquarium can be simple or elaborate. A water dish is a must. It should be large enough to hold one or two fish and also your snake, because some snakes like to curl up in the water from time to time. You can cover the bottom of the aquarium with either gravel or newspaper. I prefer the latter, because it makes cleaning much easier. Just remove the soiled newspaper and replace it with fresh. Snake feces should not be allowed to accumulate, and the simpler it is to remove them, the less you will tend to neglect this important chore.

Snakes, like most living creatures, want privacy occasionally, and the tank should have either a box (like a cigar box) with a small hole cut into it, or some rocks under which the snake can crawl. In addition, some branches for the snake to coil on will make life more interesting.

Shedding

Snakes molt regularly. This is part of their normal growth process and is nothing to be alarmed about. Before shedding its skin, a snake's eyes become cloudy white, and its skin loses its luster. A snake will usually have no difficulty shedding. Sometimes, however, it will need your help. It may be necessary to use a pair of round-tipped tweezers to remove some of the skin. Those used by postage stamp collectors are ideal. The snake will also need a rock to rub against; be sure to supply one if one is not already in the aquarium.

Ailments

Respiratory infections and mouth rot are the two most common ailments of snakes in captivity. The symptoms of respiratory infection are loss of appetite and mucous discharge from the nostrils. Warmth is extremely important. Some veterinarians are experienced with snakes, and it may be necessary to call for professional treatment.

Mouth rot is a serious bacterial infection that attacks a snake around its mouth and in the respiratory tract. In its later stages, it also attacks bone tissue and teeth. It is difficult to treat. Your pet shop may have a mouthwash to be used for the treatment of mouth rot, and if so, the instructions should be followed carefully. These usually require regular swabbing of the infected areas. Ask your veterinarian for further information.

Bites

Some snakes bite. Garter snakes will bite if they are handled roughly or if they are frightened. Once a snake becomes accustomed to your touch, you will probably have no trouble holding it. Until it is comfortable with you, though, it is a good idea to wear gloves. The best way to handle a snake is to grip it firmly with one hand right below the head and support it near the tip of its tail with the other hand.

LIZARDS

Although there are over two thousand species of lizard in the world, only a handful are available as pets. The most popular of all lizards is the Carolina anole, more popularly known as the American chameleon, or just plain chameleon.

Chameleons are small enough to permit easy handling and are fascinating to watch. Depending on lighting, temperature, and the chameleon's state of mind, it will change color from shades of green to gray to brown. Generally, it is bright green or brown during the day and a pale apple green with a paler underbelly at night.

One of the thousands of lizard species found in the world is this Armadillo lizard, sometimes found in pet shops. (*Patricia F. Fishtein*)

Housing

The best place to house a chameleon is in a glass aquarium. Since little water is kept in a chameleon's aquarium, technically it is a terrarium. The terrarium's furnishings should include a few rocks and branches for your chameleon to climb on, a covering of sand or fine gravel, and a couple of house plants. If you are keeping just one or two of these creatures, a small (5-gallon) tank is quite adequate. It should be kept near a sunny window because anoles love the sun. Since their normal temperature range lies between 50 and 95 degrees, it is not necessary to equip the terrarium with a light bulb or other heating device, although it is acceptable to do so. Your chameleon will be more active at higher temperatures.

Chameleons are excellent jumpers and climbers, so, unless you want to come home one day to an empty terrarium, be sure to buy or make a snug-fitting mesh cover for it.

Feeding

Don't be concerned if your chameleon doesn't eat after you've brought it home. After all, it has been moved from a place where it was comfortable and presumably adjusted, into an entirely new environment; it is apt to be a bit edgy. Some chameleons can go for one or two weeks without eating, and be perfectly all right. When a chameleon does eat, it prefers live food. Anything from flies, mosquitoes, small crickets, and grasshoppers to mealworms will do.

If you are a country person, you should have no trouble finding food for your chameleon in your garden. If you do not live in the country, you have to arrange to feed your pet by buying food from the local pet shop.

If you have the time, you can probably fool your chameleon into taking morsels of meat or ground beef. You can try this by impaling a small piece of meat on the end of a thin wire and jiggling it to make it appear alive and kicking. Your pet may not learn at the outset that the morsel you are dangling is good tasting, so you will have to be patient. He may not take the food at all, and it may be necessary to revert to live food, but it is worth a try.

Chameleons need water as well as food. They prefer to get their water from moist leaves in the terrarium. Although a small water dish is a good idea, it is also necessary to spray the plants every day with lukewarm water.

Once your pet becomes accustomed to you, it may be possible to hand-feed it. First, plan to spend several days gaining its confidence by stroking it gently under its chin with your forefinger. Chameleons like that. Once it gets used to stroking, hold a mealworm or small insect, such as a cricket or grasshopper, and try to entice your pet into having a snack.

Like many other reptiles, chameleons molt periodically by shedding their old skin, under which a new and attractive covering has grown.

Breeding

Chameleons can be bred easily in captivity, but they are not very good parents. Male chameleons are very territorial and will fight if there are two or more males in the same terrarium.

To determine the sex of your chameleon, place a mirror in front of your pet. If it's a male, he will inflate his dewlap —a fold of skin below the chin—when he sees his reflection and prepare to attack by doing a little dance toward the mirror. A female will ignore her reflection in the mirror.

Once you have determined that you have a pair of

anoles, you can try to breed them. The most important rules are that they be well fed and healthy.

If you intend to breed chameleons, you should place some leaves in a corner of the terrarium and inspect underneath them periodically. The female lays an average of three or four eggs during the summer months. They are very small, about ½ inch long, and are either pale green or brown. Once the female has laid them, her job as a mother is over, and neither she nor her mate will pay much attention to them. It is best, therefore, to move the eggs carefully to another home. A small glass aquarium with sand and leaves at the bottom will do. It should be kept in a warm location. Mound up the sand, place the eggs on the mound, cover with moistened leaves, and inspect the incubator daily. The eggs will hatch in one to two months.

After the fry (baby chameleons) have hatched, they can be fed a mixture of 1 cup warm water to 1 teaspoon of honey with a small eyedropper. They can also be fed small pieces of meat or ground beef on the end of a thin wire. In about two weeks the offspring will be better-equipped to fend for themselves and can be fed small flies and insects.

If you live in the country and have small flies in your house, feeding can be facilitated by putting a piece of peeled orange or apple in the terrarium. These are likely to attract the flies, and you will be surprised to learn how agile even a baby chameleon can be when foraging for a live meal.

Chameleons live to a ripe old age of four to five years in captivity and rarely get sick. If they are kept warm and well fed, there should be no problems. If your chameleon acts listless, doesn't change color as often as usual, and displays cold symptoms, the best treatment is to raise the temperature in the terrarium by putting in a light bulb and keeping it on. The temperature should be checked periodically. Try to have it close to 85 degrees.

OTHER LIZARDS

Two interesting lizards that make nice house pets are the chuckawalla and the iguana. The former can be tamed to the point where it will climb onto your hand searching for food.

Both the chuckawalla and the iguana are easier to feed than most reptiles because they can survive on a vegetarian diet, which should include lettuce, grass clippings, dandelion leaves, pieces of fruit, such as apple and banana, and flowers, such as dandelions. Although not essential, it is desirable to supplement their diet with mealworms once or twice a week.

Since the chuckawalla and iguana are considerably larger than chameleons (the chuckawalla can grow to over a foot in length), it will be necessary to have a large terrarium to house these animals. A 20-gallon fish tank is

An iguana. These lizards make interesting house pets. (*American Museum of Natural History*)

probably the best housing you can obtain. A secure mesh cover is also needed.

The tank should be furnished with a layer of sand, a basking rock, some artificial plants (real ones are likely to be eaten), a piece of wood for climbing, and a small water dish. Direct sunshine and a secluded shaded area for privacy are also necessary. If direct sun is not available, a light bulb to simulate sunshine can be used. These two lizards are very difficult to breed in captivity. Their ailments are similar to those mentioned earlier for lizards.

TURTLES

Most turtles sold in American pet shops are red-eared sliders. Sliders are aquatic; they require an aquarium half-filled with water, and rocks the turtle can climb up on when it comes out of the water. You also need a pump and filter for the aquarium; if you don't use them, the water will become foul, producing a terrible odor. Even with a pump and filter, frequent cleaning of the aquarium will be necessary.

. Another requirement of aquatic turtles is live food. They will not thrive on anything else. Some pet shops sell feeder goldfish, which can be obtained for as little as two dollars for twenty-five fish. An average-sized turtle (4 or 5 inches long) will consume five or six goldfish per week. If you are going to keep goldfish around for feeding purposes, you will need a separate aquarium for them.

In addition to goldfish, you can also try feeding your turtle earthworms, tubifex worms, flies, and small crickets and grasshoppers in season.

Box turtles are sometimes available in pet shops. They are primarily terrestrial and therefore don't need an aquarium with a substantial amount of water in it. Another advantage to terrestrial turtles (technically called *tor-*

This turtle, a red-eared slider, is frequently found in pet shops. (*American Museum of Natural History*)

toises) is that they are omniverous and can live on a vegetarian diet consisting of fruits (apple, banana, berries) and vegetables (lettuce, spinach, other greens). In addition, they will also eat new dandelion leaves, grass clippings, and a host of other plant material. They will also enjoy a piece of lean meat and, as a special treat, a few mealworms.

FROGS, TOADS, SALAMANDERS, NEWTS

These amphibians are grouped together because they thrive in similar surroundings. All require moisture and a cool environment. A long aquarium with a little water and a woodland area with twigs, soil, branches, leaves, and some rocks will provide a setting similar to the natural surroundings of these creatures.

All commercially available amphibians can learn to take fresh meat, finely cut fish, or ground beef occasionally, but you must be prepared to provide a diet of live food, such as earthworms, crickets, flies, and mealworms.

Since amphibians do not have scales to protect them from moisture loss, they must be kept out of direct sunlight and should not be handled for any length of time. If you do handle your amphibian, moisten your hands first and keep them damp until you put the animal back.

It is a good idea to have a spare tank on hand so you can transfer your pets to it during one of the frequent housecleanings that will be required.

The best temperature range for amphibians is 60 to 70 degrees. Some amphibians tolerate higher temperatures, but they won't be happy about it.

6

FISH

GENERAL INFORMATION

You can buy a goldfish bowl, a few goldfish, and some fish food for less than five dollars; or you can have a marine aquarium with exotic saltwater fish, rocks, and associated filtering and aerating equipment for thousands of dollars.

One reason for the explosive growth in the popularity of fish in the home is that one can start modestly and then expand.

There are literally scores of different fish available for the home aquarium, many as different as night and day. There are the colorful live-bearing guppies, fascinating egg-laying betas, blind cave fish, and many others, varying in coloring, size, swimming habits, and personality.

Libraries, bookshops, and pet stores are full of books written about the care, raising, feeding, and breeding of fish. It is evident that in a book of this nature we can only skim the surface, whetting the fish fancier's appetite for more. What we can do is provide the fundamentals fairly well. First, we will cover general information, then we'll go into more detail.

FISH TANKS

In general, it is not desirable to put a fish in a bowl. Fish, like most living creatures, must have oxygen to survive. Oxygen is absorbed from the air that is in contact with the surface of the water. Therefore it stands to reason that the larger the surface area of the water, the greater the supply of oxygen. An average-sized aquarium fish requires about 9 square inches of surface area in order to have enough oxygen to survive. Most goldfish bowls have little more than that available. Although some fish can survive under marginal conditions, it is obvious that if you put more than the minimum number of fish in a bowl, they won't last long—they will suffocate from lack of oxygen.

So rule number one is: Plan on buying a standard rectangular aquarium if you are going to raise fish in your home. Although there are different kinds of aquaria available, the best is of glass and stainless steel. This is the most problem free, the most durable, and the safest to use.

Since many fish are jumpers, you will need some kind of covering for the top of your aquarium. Here, too, your choices are numerous. You can use glass, plastic, mesh, or a one-piece stainless steel covering with reflector lights built in. These serve the dual purpose of providing protection for the fish as well as light. They also have cutouts in the top through which accessory equipment such as thermometers, filters, aerators, and heaters can be attached.

Since most of the fish available for home aquaria come from warm-water regions of the earth, it is necessary to keep the temperature of the water in the vicinity of 75 degrees; the only way to do so consistently is with an aquarium heater. It is also necessary to monitor the temperature of the water, and this is done with a thermometer suitable for use in an aquarium.

Waste products are disposed of through various types of filtering equipment, which are generally driven by a pump. The pump serves to force air into the water. Aeration increases the oxygen content of the water and makes it possible to have more fish in the tank.

There are two general types of pump available—diaphragm and piston. A piston pump is generally more powerful and can be used to aerate and filter several tanks simultaneously. Diaphragm pumps are generally less expensive and are recommended for the beginner.

Filtering equipment contains charcoal to purify the water and fibrous material to filter out waste products. These filters are housed in a plastic container. They can be placed either inside the aquarium or hung on the outside. Another type of filter is available which is installed under the gravel. For the sake of simplicity, I prefer the outside filter.

Heaters with a thermostat attachment are sold in all pet stores carrying fish and are relatively inexpensive. They contain a device which signals the heater to operate when the water reaches a certain temperature.

One of the delights of having an aquarium is that very attractive aquatic plants can be obtained inexpensively. An entire book could be written about aquarium plants alone. These plants can be either the floating variety or the kind with roots. If you are going to have plants on the floor of your aquarium, you will need something to hold them down. Gravel is ideally suited for such a purpose. Since gravel comes in an assortment of colors, it is also more pleasing to the eye than the slate bottoms on most fish tanks. A dramatic effect can be obtained if you experiment with different colors.

Your plants should have at least ten hours a day of incandescent light or twelve hours of fluorescent light. Direct sun is not recommended. The most popular of the

freshwater aquarium plants are vallisneria, sagittaria, ana-
charis, and cabomba. An Amazon sword plant is more
expensive, but highly dramatic as the centerpiece of your
aquarium. The choice and placement of plants are largely
a matter of taste, and you will enjoy arranging and rear-
ranging. Start modestly, though.

You will probably want to decorate your aquarium with
some rocks or other ornaments. Safe, chemically-stable
ornaments are plentiful in pet shops. Rocks can be dangerous; unless you are knowledgeable about their chemical content and stability, it is best to purchase these as well
in a pet shop. Be sure you wash them thoroughly before
putting them into the tank.

Last but not least: the kind of water you use is crucial
to the success of your tank. Freshly-drawn tap water is not
safe in most areas. It generally contains chlorine, which is
harmful to most fish.

It is necessary, therefore, to let tap water stand two or
three days before putting it into a tank. In that time the
chlorine will evaporate. As an alternative, pet shops carry
tablets which will dechlorinate water in a very short time.
Read the instructions carefully before using.

Two other water-related factors are of some impor-
tance to aquarists. One is hardness, the other acidity/alka-
linity of the water.

Most water contains some minerals. The greater the
mineral content, the harder the water. Hardness is rarely
a problem where municipal water supplies are concerned.
But if your water source is a well, chances are the water
is harder than it should be to maintain fish. Most pet
stores sell kits with which mineral content can be mea-
sured easily. The kit will indicate how much softener you
will have to add to your water.

Acidity or alkalinity is expressed in terms of pH on a
scale from 0 to 14. Water with a pH of 7.0 is neutral. PH

values below 7.0 indicate acid water, and above 7.0, alkaline. A range between 6.5 and 7.7 is suitable for almost all freshwater tropical fish. PH testing kits can be purchased inexpensively at your pet shop, together with chemicals which enable you to treat the water, if treatment is required.

While we are on the subject of water, two problems that plague many aquarists are cloudy water and green water.

Cloudy water is caused by excessive waste materials in the tank or by overfeeding. In both cases, certain types of bacteria multiply rapidly, to the point where it appears that milk has been added to the water. This is both unsightly and dangerous to the fish.

The best remedy for cloudy water is to prevent it. Do not overfeed the fish. Food should be consumed within five minutes of feeding. Anything left over represents an excess. Second, make sure the filter is working properly and is cleaned regularly. Just remove filtering material and charcoal and rinse under running water.

If there is waste material on the gravel that is not being removed by the filter, a dip tube should be used for supplementary cleaning. A dip tube is an inexpensive siphon-like device that enables you to scoop waste materials from the bottom of the tank for easy disposal.

A thorough cleaning of the tank, followed by a partial water change will help rid your tank of cloudy water.

Green water is caused by minute plants called algae, which are often brought in with aquarium plants; they can also be airborne. Algae multiply rapidly in light, especially direct sunlight, and a green tank is an indication that the light is too strong, or that you are illuminating your tank for too long a time.

Reduce the amount of light in the tank and partially change the water. Some fish eat algae. One or two of these fish in an aquarium will help control the green water situation. Black or green mollies and and suckermouth catfish are the best of the algae eaters.

FOODS

When I first started raising tropical fish, some thirty years ago, frozen food was difficult to obtain, and when one of my suppliers received a shipment of frozen brine shrimp or daphnia, I quickly purchased as much as I could afford and stored it in my freezer at home. Storing fish food at home was generally a sore point with my wife. In addition to having fish food in the freezer, I kept live food, usually tubifex worms, in the refrigerator, and more than once my wife opened the refrigerator door and let out a loud shriek when she saw the worms. If you want to raise large, healthy, happy fish, this is the price you must pay.

Fish food is available either dried, frozen, or live. Live is best, and generally includes tubifex worms, daphnia, brine shrimp, bloodworms, or other fish. Live tubifex worms should be kept in a closed container, with just enough water to cover the ball of worms. The worms must be stirred every day, gently breaking up the ball under cold running water to wash away waste products. After a thorough rinsing, some of the clean worms can be fed to the fish.

Baby fish (fry) can be fed either newly-hatched brine shrimp or chopped tubifex worms. This can be done by placing several worms on a small piece of solid sheet plastic and using a single-edge razor blade to chop the worms fine. These are fed to the babies daily. Tubifex worms are very nutritious and one of the best foods you can give aquarium fish.

Various frozen fish foods are available in most pet stores, and you can experiment with these until you discover the preferences of your fish. The same applies to the many dried foods that are currently available. As a special treat, you can also try chopped raw fish or shrimp.

DISEASES

Tropical fish are subject to a wide range of ailments, some understood, some not. A pet shop owner with whom I did a considerable amount of business once told me when I complained of the death of a favorite black mollie of mine, "Fish die." That sums it up, and it is not advisable for an aquarist to get too attached to his fish. On the average, you can expect a healthy fish to live no longer than two years.

You would think that in the protected environment of a home aquarium fish wouldn't become ill. But they do. Because new plants, fish, and even water are introduced at regular intervals, all too often the new addition brings something in with it.

It is, therefore, best to keep new fish and plants separated for a week to ten days before adding them to a community tank (a tank containing a number of compatible fishes). It's not a foolproof method, but it will help.

It is also a good idea to watch a fish carefully before you buy it. Don't ask the pet store attendant to choose a fish for you. Do it yourself. Observe the fish carefully. It should not have any white spots on it, or white growths in the corner of its mouth, and it should swim freely. One symptom of a sick fish is that it "shimmies"—it remains in one place and wags its body back and forth. It looks as if it has chills. Make sure the fish does not scratch itself against rocks or plants; this is an indication that some parasite on or under its scales is causing irritation. As a matter of fact, if any fish in a tank shows these symptoms, it is not a good idea to buy anything from that tank. If there are dead fish in a tank, you must certainly not buy a fish from the same tank.

Be selective; don't be hasty; and you will prevent lots of trouble before it starts.

It is also a good idea to check the general condition of all the tanks in the store before you decide to buy. Are they clean and well cared for? Are there accumulations of green or brown algae on the front of the tanks? If there are, then the maintenance program in the shop is not good.

If you take these precuations, you will reduce the likelihood of disease considerably. Despite all precautions, however, it is still possible to have sick fish. The most common aquarium disease is *ick*. This is the appearance of white spots on the fins and body of a fish. This disease is caused by a parasite and can be treated with various ick remedies now available in pet stores. Raising the temperature in the tank to around 85 degrees for several days will accelerate the treatment.

Fish are attacked by various fungi and bacterial diseases that sometimes cause the fins or tail to rot. Mouth fungus is characterized by the appearance of a cottony white substance in the corners of the mouth. In its advanced stages it may fill the mouth entirely. Fish stores have various antibiotic remedies for rot and fungus, and instructions should be followed.

GOLDFISH

Raising and breeding goldfish has increased in popularity in recent years. Rare and exotic varieties of goldfish have been developed, ranging from the bubble-eyed types to black moors, calicos, and lionheads. Goldfish can be purchased for as little as ten cents or as much as hundreds of

A tankful of goldfish can make a beautiful display. They are active and fun to watch. (*American Museum of Natural History*)

dollars. Many books have been written about raising different varieties of this interesting species.

Generally speaking, goldfish and tropical fish, whether they are freshwater or marine, are incompatible. Goldfish are larger and more aggressive and will eat tropical fish. Few of the popular standard types of freshwater tropicals would survive long in a tankful of goldfish. There are also different temperature requirements. Goldfish are comfortable in cold water, at temperatures in which no tropical fish could survive. Their upper limit is about 65 degrees, which is the lower range for tropicals.

Because of their temperature tolerance, a tank of goldfish doesn't need a heater. On the contrary, it is desirable in the summertime to keep the temperature down. This is usually done by vigorous aeration and, because this accelerates evaporation rate, by the frequent addition of cooler water.

Goldfish are relatively large fish, so they need a large

tank. Filtering and aeration are necessary both to keep the tank clean and to increase the oxygen supply in the water.

Goldfish eat anything tropical fish eat, including dried, frozen, and live foods available in pet shops. Frozen or live food is more nutritious than dried food, so all fish should be given as much of the former as possible.

THE FRESHWATER COMMUNITY TANK

The best project for a beginning aquarist is a community tank—a selection of different varieties, preferably with differing habits, coloring, and breeding characteristics, which are compatible with one another, together in one tank. In general, the fish selected should be of the same or similar size since larger fish have the unfortunate habit of eating smaller ones.

There are two basic tropical fish categories: live-bearers and egg-layers.

There are four groups of live-bearers—guppies, platys, swordtails, and mollies. Within each group there are color variations, as well as differences in the size and shape of fins. Of the live-bearers, guppies exhibit the most variety in terms of coloring, shape, and length of tail. Guppy enthusiasts spend great sums of money for fine and highly distinctive pairs of good guppies.

On the other hand, a pair of so-called common guppies, with good coloring and shape, can be purchased for under a dollar. This explains why guppies are probably the most popular of all aquarium fishes.

Next in order of interest are the mollies. Most mollies are solid black, and some have large saillike fins (called sailfins) with lyre-shaped tails.

Platys and swordtails come in many colors, including gold, orange, variegated, and various combinations of these.

A male guppy is courting the female. The small arrow points to the gonopodium, which is pointing forward. (*American Museum of Natural History*)

In general, all live-bearers are compatible and can be kept in a community tank.

Egg-Layers

By far the majority of aquarium fishes are the egg-laying type and, although their individual breeding habits differ significantly, they are generally grouped together.

Tetras, of which there are several interesting varieties, are compatible with most other aquarium fishes. The most popular and attractive are neons, cardinals, glowlights, and head-and-taillight tetras. These fish are characterized by bright reflecting areas. The neons and cardinals, for example, have a brilliant blue and red stripe running horizontally along the length of their bodies, which appears to glow. Glowlights have a spot which glows, and head-and-taillights, as the name implies, have two such spots. Tetras are most beautiful when seen in schools. They remain together in a tank, and the more of a single variety you have, the more dramatic the effect. You should have at least three of one kind.

Barbs, like tetras, are schooling fish. Perhaps the most attractive of the barbs is the sumatranus, which is colored light gold, with a stunning contrast of deep brown horizontal stripes. Also included in this popular group are rasboras and zebra danios, which are striped, and the lighter, stripeless, pearl danios. The danios are the most active of all aquarium fishes; they are constantly in motion —darting and flitting through the tank, chasing each other around at a sometimes madcap pace. They, too, are highly compatible fish and an important addition to any community tank.

Angel fish and the more expensive, more regal discus fish, are the stately members of the community aquarium. They are occasionally aggressive but rarely cause much damage. Though not very active, they are among the most beautiful of the aquarium fishes and often seem to be floating in the water, almost as if they were painted in place.

Every community tank needs at least one scavenger—

An angel fish, one of the most popular of the egg-layers. (*Patricia F. Fishtein*)

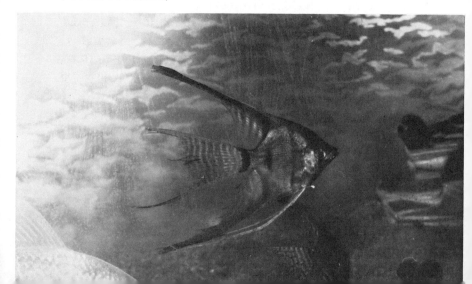

a fish that feeds off the bottom of the tank, picking up scraps that have fallen to the bottom, digging and foraging in the gravel for food that would otherwise decay and eventually foul the tank. Catfish are the best scavengers. They are very active and amusing to watch, periodically darting wildly to the top of the aquarium and scooting back down again just as quickly. Of the numerous varities of catfish, the most common is the green catfish.

BUBBLE NEST BUILDERS

Some egg-layers are especially interesting because they are bubble-nest builders. The males build nests of small bubbles, at the surface of the water. These are produced by surrounding a bit of air with a mucuslike substance from the male's mouth. Fertilized eggs are taken by the male in his mouth and deposited in the nest. The bubble-nest builders are less suited to the community tank than other egg-layers. The most prominent of the bubble-nest builders are betas, or Siamese fighting fish, and gouramis, the most common of which are blue and kissing gouramis.

A single male beta can be kept in a community tank with satisfactory results, but two or more males will fight viciously with each other. Female betas can be kept in a community tank, but if a male is placed in with them, the male will attack them, unless they are breeding.

Gouramis can be kept with other tropical fishes, but since these fishes can grow to be 6 inches long, they must be kept with fish of the same size. If not, the smaller fish will soon become gourami food.

Breeding

Many books have been written about breeding tropical fish, and it should be evident that in a book of this nature only a very simple treatment of the subject can be given.

The easiest fish to breed are the live-bearers. All you

have to do is feed the pair well with plenty of fresh (live and frozen) food, and nature will take care of the rest. The sex of live-bearers is easy to distinguish. The males are generally sleeker and are sometimes, as in the case of guppies, more colorful. The males have a gonopodium, equivalent to a penis, which is a modified fin on the lower abdomen, elongated and tubular. It normally points toward the tail fin, but it can be pivoted 180 degrees to point in the forward direction. The male can swing the gonopodium to right and left, making this little organ even more versatile.

It is through the gonopodium that sperm are delivered to the female's vent. Fry (baby fish) develop within the female, and in a matter of about three weeks, anywhere from five to twenty-five fully developed little fishes are dropped. During the gestation period, the female's body swells, and a dark spot near her vent, called the gravid spot, grows. When the female is ready to drop her young, her lower abdomen is not only enlarged, but almost square. It does not take long for even a beginner to recognize when the birth is about to take place.

There are various ways to save the fry from being eaten by the other fish in the tank. Newborn fry instinctively dart for plants when they are born, and if an aquarium has an abundance of thick plants, the chances of survival are fairly good.

A much better method involves isolating the female when she is ready to drop her young. Breeders keep well-planted tanks available for this purpose, and as soon as the female has completed dropping her fry, she is removed, leaving the offspring in a tank by themselves.

For the casual breeder who does not have a separate tank, breeding traps are available. These are plastic containers that are hung inside the aquarium. The bottom is slotted, and as fry are dropped they fall through the slots into a separate compartment. This is necessary because baby fish are great delicacies, even to their mother, and if not protected and kept separate, they will probably be eaten by her—unless she is kept very well fed. Once the mother has finished dropping her young she is removed, and the slotted partition is taken out to give the fry as much room in the breeding trap as possible. Babies may be fed dry food for fry or newly-hatched brine shrimp. Brine shrimp eggs are available in most pet shops, and the eggs can easily be hatched in homemade saltwater. Be sure not to use iodized salt. Brine shrimp will not hatch in iodized-saltwater. After they begin to hatch, the shrimp can be attracted to one side of the container by placing an incandescent light bulb nearby. They are then removed with an eyedropper and deposited in the breeding trap. Fry love them.

When the baby fish are about half an inch long, they can be moved and will generally fend for themselves in a community tank, unless you have relatively large fish—in which case half-inch fish are just about bite size!

Egg-layers are generally more difficult to breed, and it is best to have a separate tank and a known pair for this purpose. Except for betas, which are easily distinguishable (the male has much larger, more colorful fins), it is harder to tell the sex of egg-layers. If you are interested in breeding a particular variety, it is best to start by asking your pet shop owner to sell you a pair of breeders. If he can't help you, one of the scores of specialized books available on aquarium fish as a hobby will prove helpful. These can be found in almost any public library or bookstore.

SALTWATER FISHES

Generally speaking, marine (saltwater) aquaria are more

expensive and more difficult to keep than freshwater ones.

A marine aquarium requires both an outside and an inside filter which is submerged under the gravel in the tank. Plants are not used in marine aquaria, but some rocks and coral can be added.

A marine aquarium will support only about one-third the number of fish that a comparable freshwater aquarium can sustain. Saltwater chemistry differs considerably from that of freshwater. The former fouls much more easily and requires a more delicate chemical balance.

Saltwater fish are much more expensive than freshwater tropicals, and it is advisable for a beginner to start with an inexpensive freshwater tropical setup to gain experience.

A sea horse, one of the most exotic of marine aquarium fishes. They are fussy eaters and will survive only if given a diet of live food. (*American Museum of Natural History*)

A pet shop which carries saltwater fish will also stock the salt needed to convert freshwater to saltwater. In addition, the same shop will sell you a hygrometer, an instrument that measures the density of the water, so that you will know when more freshwater has to be added or when your aquarium needs salt.

Until you have gained experience, it is a good idea to start with relatively inexpensive saltwater fish such as dominoes, damsels, and blue devils, which may be purchased for about two dollars each. When one considers that a small neon tetra for a freshwater tank can be obtained for about twenty cents, it becomes apparent that a saltwater tank can be an expensive proposition.

On the other hand, some of the most exotic creatures on the planet can be seen in marine aquaria. Among these are anemones, sea horses, threadfish, saltwater angels, and many more.

Saltwater fishes are generally fussy eaters, and one area of possible difficulty with a marine aquarium is feeding. In general, fresh food is required. That means either live or frozen. Diet should be varied, too. Dry food is unacceptable and will only contribute to fouling the water, so don't even try using it.

Although keeping marine fishes can be a very exciting hobby, it is not recommended for beginners.

7
MONKEYS

Years ago, before the United States government placed severe restrictions on the wholesale importation of monkeys, these exotic animals were fairly popular as house pets. Unfortunately, monkeys don't do well in the home; they are susceptible to many diseases, including hepatitis, yellow fever, and a wide range of respiratory infections, including influenza and pneumonia, which can be caught from humans. Because the average pet owner doesn't know enough about the complex dietetic requirements of primates, many monkeys do not thrive as house pets because of nutritional deficiencies.

Monkeys are naturally gregarious and require their own kind to keep them company. If kept alone they are likely to be lonely and brood a good deal of the time. As an added disadvantage, monkeys are very strong and can do a great deal of damage in a very short time.

Some years ago I had a woolly monkey as a house pet. When I first purchased her she couldn't have been more than 8 inches long from the top of her head to the base of her tail. I bought a large birdcage for her to live in, but within two weeks she had shaken it to pieces by swinging from one side of the cage to the other. I bought a larger,

100

sturdier cage, and for a while it seemed strong enough. One day I came home from an outing with the family to find our woolly monkey sitting on the kitchen floor, a half-eaten banana in one hand, an apple in the other. Nearby was an overturned fruit bowl, and chewed-up fruit and monkey droppings were strewn all over the house.

To contain her, I finally had to build a cage using two-by-fours and steel bars. Mazeltov, our monkey, lived with us for five years and grew to be like one of the family. She was very bright and impressed us with some of her tricks, but we could never housebreak her, so taking her out of the cage was always an adventure.

Although the normal lifespan of monkeys can be as much as twenty-five years, most pet monkeys live no longer than five years and frequently much less.

Another disadvantage of having monkeys as pets is that as they approach maturity they become more and more disagreeable and are inclined to bite even the people they love. Consequently, many pet monkeys are disposed of by their owners once they become difficult to handle.

In spite of the fact that the importation of monkeys has decreased considerably in recent years, a great many animals are still brought into the country for laboratory work. Some of these creatures occasionally become available to the pet shop trade. For those who are still interested in monkeys as pets, the following is a brief description of those most commonly found in pet shops and of their requirements when raised as pets.

WOOLLIES

Our woolly was very loving when she was young. As she grew older, larger, and stronger, however, she was inclined to have temper tantrums, particularly when something frightened her. The first time our new golden retriever approached her cage, she fell to the bottom of the cage and screamed hysterically until we removed the dog from her sight.

Another problem we had with her was that she was epileptic and suffered frequent seizures, which were very painful for us to watch.

Maz, as we called her, was very expensive to feed. Although she ate table scraps, including meats and vegetables, her favorite foods were fruits and nuts. Even ten years ago these were quite costly to purchase. She could go through 5 or 6 pounds of fruit a week. During the summer months we would take her outside on a leash, where she relished catching and eating insects.

SPIDER MONKEYS

These are appropriately named. They have long limbs and tails, and actually do resemble spiders. A great deal of space is required to house spiders because they are very active. Since they are gregarious as well, at least two of a kind are required if they are to be happy. Spiders are inclined to bite even the hand that feeds them with their sharp little teeth.

A brown spider monkey. (*American Museum of Natural History*)

SQUIRREL MONKEYS

Squirrel monkeys are very high-strung and delicate and are not generally hardy, being susceptible to a great many kinds of viral infections. They seldom live more than two years in the home and must have the companionship of at least one more squirrel monkey, not necessarily of the opposite sex.

8

SKUNKS

Many pet shops sell descented skunks, but it should be pointed out that even without their scent glands skunks can be formidable animals to have around. They have sharp teeth and long, powerful claws that can dig into upholstered furniture, carpeting, or human flesh with equal ferocity.

Skunks are easily frightened, and even one which has become accustomed to its owner is not above giving a bite or two or a few deep claw marks.

Disadvantages aside, skunks can be exotic, conversation-piece pets who are docile and affectionate, especially if raised from infancy. Skunks do not take well to confinement, however, and they become very grouchy if they are kept in a cage for too long.

Skunks are difficult, if not impossible, to housebreak, and reports that they can be trained to use a litter box are highly exaggerated. Consequently they cannot be given the run of the house. They must also be kept away from household furnishings that they will use for nest building.

Disregarding the few exceptions, skunks are not recommended as house pets because most of them are generally destructive and aggressive. For those animal lovers who are gluttons for punishment, however, some pertinent facts about skunk-keeping follow.

Skunks are nocturnal, and it is very difficult to untrain them because their inclinations toward nighttime activity are very strong. In the wild, skunks hibernate during the winter months, and a pet skunk will grow lethargic as winter approaches, even though it will not actually go into hibernation. In winter, therefore, skunks should not be overfed, because they will grow fat and become even more lethargic.

In the wild, skunks eat rodents, insects, wild vegetation, turtle eggs, and an occasional chicken. In captivity, skunks will eat fruits, such as apples, grapes, bananas; vegetables, such as carrots; and nuts, canned dog and cat food, chicken, bread, and cereals. They also like whole milk, but since that can give them serious diarrhea, it is not recommended.

A skunk can be kept in a large cage or box, but it will need a nesting area into which it can retire for privacy. A box about the length of the animal, with a hole it can barely get through is required for nesting. It should contain soft material, such as shredded paper, kitty litter, or wood chips.

Most skunks are fairly uninteresting animals in captivity. They are much more useful to humanity in the wild, where they destroy rodents and insects.

9
DOGS

Of all the animals discussed in this book, dogs are among the most rewarding and probably the most demanding, in terms of both care and cost. Dogs must be trained and fed and must receive regular veterinary attention. If you live in an urban area they must be walked regularly, rain or shine, and in some cities, such as New York, they must also be picked up after. Some dogs are very temperamental, and others bark excessively and can be an awful nuisance.

Having covered the disadvantages, let me add that no animal I know of can consistently be more of a friend and companion than a dog. In some cases, a dog can be a playmate, as well.

In their ten-thousand-year association with humans, dogs have been used for hunting, guarding, racing, leading the blind, searching out foods (such as truffles), and even assisting narcotics agents to find illegally concealed drugs.

There are more than four hundred different dog pedigrees worldwide and over one hundred recognized breeds in the United States. Of the estimated 150 million dogs on earth, more than 30 million reside in this country.

Dogs not only vary in temperament and behavior, they

vary in size and shape as well. The tiny chihuahua weighs about 1½ pounds full grown, whereas a full-grown St. Bernard weighs 200 pounds.

The choice of a dog should depend on your requirements and the facilities available. Don't pick a dog simply because it is cute and cuddly, or the runt of a litter, or because it will be destroyed if you don't give it a home. In the long run, both of you will be unhappy if a dog is chosen for the wrong reasons.

First, the dog you choose should fit comfortably into your home. A St. Bernard puppy may be a very lovely lapdog for a while, but when fully grown it will probably outweigh you. Unless it has a large area to live in and gets

The author with his cairn terrier, Toby. (*Steve Curreri*)

Toby removing the cover from a can of tennis balls. (*Steve Curreri*)

sufficient exercise, you will not be doing justice to the animal or yourself.

Second, the choice should depend on your requirements. Is your pet to be a watchdog? If so, you will want a dog that barks, such as a terrier, or one that is protective, such as a German shepherd.

If you want a lapdog, then poodles and terriers are probably best. Of all the dogs I have ever had, none has been more fun than Toby, my cairn terrier. He plays ball, retrieves, loves to have his belly rubbed, and has learned to remove the cover from a can of tennis balls when he wants to play.

The retriever is the gentlest of dogs. Labrador and golden retrievers are unusually mild-mannered and consequently are very good with children.

Before you choose a dog, then, ask yourself what you

108

require of it, then find one that matches your facilities and your needs.

Once you have decided what kind of dog you want, there are several ways to go about obtaining it. If you want a purebred, the best thing to do is to go to a breeder specializing in that breed. Make certain the breeder is reputable. Ask about him or her among your friends and check with the local Better Business Bureau to be sure there have been no complaints against the breeder. A reliable breeder will certify that your pup has had its shots (distemper, hepatitis, and leptospirosis) and will guarantee that proper papers will be forwarded to you within several months. In addition, you should have a written agreement from the breeder to take the dog back under certain conditions; namely, that if within a certain period a veterinarian determines the dog is seriously ill, it can be returned.

Pet shops are another source of supply for pedigreed dogs. But be alert. Pet shops rely on quick turnover, and some shops are not too careful about the manner in which they look after their animals. I have seen mangy, flea-infested dogs sold by some pet shops to unsuspecting buyers. Inspect your dog carefully. Be sure there is no staining around the eyes, that all body openings are clean and show no signs of infection, that its eyes are clear, and that the animal is generally alert and playful. There should be no bare patches in its coat, and it should not scratch itself excessively. Your bill of sale should indicate what shots the dog has had and should include the same right to return the animal that a reputable breeder will give.

You can also obtain a dog through ads in the paper, from humane shelters, and from friends. Chances are these will be mixed breeds, and the first thing you should find out is a little bit about parentage, if possible. I cannot say too often that all puppies are cute and cuddly, but many of them grow up to be very large animals. It is generally too late once that happens, so try to anticipate.

Taking an animal from a friend or relative entails a special responsibility, and if the adoption doesn't work out there can be a problem. When my brother-in-law moved from New Jersey to Washington, D.C., he gave us his golden retriever. We already had a collie and a beagle and thought one pet more wouldn't matter much. Although Chuncie, our new addition, was the gentlest dog imaginable, and although he would bring the paper to me every morning (after a while I was able to ignore the fact that he slobbered on it), he had certain shortcomings my brother-in-law hadn't told us about. Chuncie had a very delicate stomach, for example, and although he consumed large quantities of food daily, he had an unfortunate habit of throwing up on a favorite rug about twice a week. Being a country dog, Chuncie also liked very much to roll on dog or horse droppings whenever he found them, which was quite often.

As a consequence, Chuncie was in the bathtub more often than he was out of it. So take heed. Before accepting an animal, learn as much as possible about it, and if feasible, hold out for an option to return it if the transaction doesn't work out.

VETERINARY CARE

A newly acquired dog should be taken to a veterinarian for an examination. Dogs can be attacked by fleas, lice, ticks, and various types of worms. A veterinarian will examine your animal and treat it, if necessary. All dogs also require periodic rabies shots. Some communities offer free rabies clinics on a regular basis, but in most instances your veterinarian will have to give your dog its shots.

FEEDING

The average pet food department in most supermarkets is larger than the baby food department. If you have a problem feeding your dog or puppy, it will most likely involve making the right choice of what to feed it. Dogs are omnivorous and will eat most meats, many kinds of grains, eggs, cheeses, and a wide assortment of vegetables. Fruit is not generally eaten, although Chuncie ate everything, including bananas, sometimes with the peel.

Puppy chows can be purchased in most food stores, but your veterinarian should be consulted for advice concerning diet for the particular breed (whether it be full or mixed) that you have.

As a general rule, a balance between dry dog food, canned food, and table scraps is most satisfactory. You will have to learn from experience what your dog's favorite foods are, but be careful not to overfeed it. My cairn terrier gained 4 pounds one winter, going from 17 to 21 pounds in just four months. A combination of his favorite foods and not enough outdoor activity caused the weight gain.

Miniature poodles are known for their intelligence, are easily trained, and don't shed. (*Marjorie Heine*)

One last word about feeding. Your veterinarian will probably tell you that puppies should be fed four or five times daily. When the puppies are ten weeks old, feedings are reduced to three times daily, and by the time your dog reaches the age of one year, this should be reduced to one feeding daily.

Vitamin and mineral supplements are available and can be added to your dog's diet, but if food intake is balanced, supplements are not necessary.

Dogs must have water. A bowl of fresh water should be available near its usual eating place and should be changed at least once daily. If your dog is permitted to roam free outdoors, water should also be accessible to it there.

HOUSING

Most pet dogs live indoors. Depending on its size, a dog can be trained to sleep on a dog bed, a blanket, a favorite chair, or your bed. Basements, cellars, or garages are unsatisfactory because they are either too hot, too cold, or too damp. Furthermore, a dog considers itself a member of the family and will feel rejected if it is kept in a separate part of the house.

Long-haired or heavy-coated dogs can be trained to live outdoors in all kinds of weather. A doghouse is generally used for this purpose. The house should contain an opening just barely large enough to admit the dog. It should be 3 to 6 inches higher than the height of the dog's head when the dog is standing, and a little longer than the dog's total length. The opening should face away from the prevailing winter winds, and a rug or blanket should be placed on the floor of the doghouse which, if possible, should be several inches above the ground. The floor covering should be checked regularly to be certain it is not wet. Forcing a dog to sleep on a cold damp surface is an invitation to illness—and inhumane, as well.

Do not house your dog in an enclosure that is much larger than the dog itself. The smaller the enclosure, the warmer it will be. The dog's body heat will help warm the house during cold weather.

GROOMING

How often to bathe and brush your dog depends on many factors. Leash dogs raised in the city will require less frequent bathing than country dogs that are allowed the run of the area. Brushing depends on hair length; short-hairs need little or no brushing.

TRAINING

It would be very nice if puppies were born housebroken, or if they self-trained, like most cats. Unfortunately, they aren't, and don't. Consequently, most dog owners are faced with the unpleasant prospect of training their dog. Actually, it isn't as bad as many people think. You need patience, newspaper, and a little determination. There are many ways to housebreak a dog. Some are cruel. I do not believe in hitting a dog when it makes a mistake. If you reward it when it does the right thing (by speaking in warm, affectionate, enthusiastic tones) and punish it when it errs (speak firmly, in a louder voice than normal. "No!" or "Bad dog!" will do it), you will probably make your point just as well as by hitting the animal.

The simplest way to housebreak a dog is to paper-train it. Confine the dog to an area which is covered with newspaper. This can be either a single room or a fenced-off area. Before long you will notice that your dog prefers to use a particular part of the room. This is generally in an area that is furthest from its food. Gradually remove the paper from the rest of the room and observe the dog. Chances are you will note a time schedule. Watch the dog carefully when you expect it to go on the paper. When it starts to do so, interrupt it, take it outside, and when it does eliminate, reward it with a kind word and a favorite morsel. If convenient, place newspaper outside your door to facilitate the transition from eliminating indoors to doing so outdoors.

The entire procedure should not take more than two or three weeks. Remember, kindness and reward will not only produce results as quickly as mistreating the animal, it will also result in an emotionally healthy, secure, and more enjoyable animal.

DISEASES

Dogs are susceptible to viral (distemper, hepatitis, rabies) and bacterial (leptospirosis) diseases. These are serious and can cause death in a dog in a short time. In addition, humans can be infected with rabies and leptospirosis. Inoculations for each of these serious diseases can be given by any veterinarian. There is little excuse for neglecting your pet by not having these important preventive shots given regularly. A reliable veterinarian will not only provide the shots, but will notify you by mail when boosters are due.

Dogs are susceptible to attacks by worms, including roundworms, tapeworms, heartworms, and hookworms. Periodic veterinary examination of stool samples and treatment if worms are present is necessary.

Ticks, fleas, mites, and lice sometimes attack dogs. Tick and flea collars are useful in preventing serious attacks, but periodic veterinary examination will help detect the presence of these parasites.

BREEDING

Male dogs can be bred at any time after they have matured. Females can be bred only when they are in heat (estrous). The reproductive cycle of the bitch (female dog) occurs in four stages: in stage one, the genitals swell and there is an accompanying flow of bright red blood. After about ten days, the color of the flow changes to lighter red. It is during this second period, which lasts about ten days, that the bitch can conceive. A third stage then occurs. It is called metestrous and lasts several days, during which the flow subsides and then stops entirely. The fourth stage lasts five months, after which the cycle begins again. Most females have two estrous cycles a year (unless, of course, they have been spayed).

If you have a female, it is best to have her spayed unless you plan to raise puppies as a vocation or avocation. It is unfair to the animal and to yourself to have unwanted litters periodically. Consult your veterinarian to find out the best age at which to have your dog spayed.

Pregnancy in the female lasts about two months, and the size of a litter depends on many factors, including dog size and breed. It takes about six weeks to wean the pups.

APPENDIX I

The reference charts which follow summarize information given in this book for all the pets described. For each pet information is listed concerning size, lifespan, housing required, food requirements, and breeding.

Understandably, material provided in chart form must be brief and is provided as a quick reference only. For additional details, consult the text.

Animal	Size at Maturity	Lifespan	Housing	Food	Breeding
American chameleon	6"–8"	2–3 yrs.	Terrarium	Live: meal-worms, flies	Fairly easy
Anole	See American chameleon				
Budgerigar	See Parakeet				
Canary	5"–6"	10–12 yrs.	Cage	Seed, song food, fruit greens, grit cuttlebone	Easy
Cat	To 20 lbs.	To 20 yrs.	Freedom of house, with litter box	Cat food with table scraps	Easy
Cavy	See Guinea pig				
Chimpanzee	Not recommended as house pet				
Cockatiel	See Lovebird				
Dog	1½–200+ lbs.	10–18+ yrs.	Run of the house, or doghouse	Dog food, table scraps	Easy
Finch	3"–6"	2–3 yrs.	Bird cage 12"×12"×12" minimum	Finch seed, cuttlebone grit, fruits, vegetables	Fairly easy

	Size	Life span	Housing	Food	Breeding
Fish	½"–6"+	1–2 yrs.	Aquarium	Dried, frozen, or live fish foods	Live-bearers: easy; egg-layers: easy to impossible
Gerbil	To 6 oz.; about 5" long	3–5 yrs.	Cage or aquarium with wire top; sleeping box	Seeds, pellets, vegetables	Easy
Guinea pig	2–3 lbs. 10"–12" long	6–8 yrs.	Box or cage 1'×3' or longer	Seeds, pellets, green vegetables	Easy
Hamster	3"–5" long, up to 5 oz.	3–4 yrs.	Same as gerbil	Same as gerbil	Easy
Iguana	To 6'	20 yrs. or more	Large wood or glass enclosure	Fruit, vegetables, worms, dog food	Difficult
Lovebird	6"–7"	About 15 yrs.	Same as parakeet	Same as parakeet, plus some sunflower seeds	Easy
Monkey	To 20 lbs.	To 25 yrs., but seldom more than 5 yrs. as house pets	Sturdy cage	Fruits, vegetables, insects seeds	Difficult to impossible

Animal	Size at Maturity	Lifespan	Housing	Food	Breeding
Mouse	6–8 oz., to 4" long	2–4 yrs.	Tank or cage, with box, wheel, bedding	Seeds, fruits, pellets, vegetables	Easy
Mynah bird	To 12"	15–20 yrs.	Large cage	Seeds, fruits, vegetables	Difficult
Parakeet	7"	8–12 yrs.	Same as for Finch	Parakeet seed, cuttlebone, grit, condition food, fruit, vegetables	Easy
Parrot	To 1' or more	50 years or more	Large cage	Seeds, fruit, vegetables, worms, cuttlebone	Difficult
Rabbit	8–15 lbs.	6–8 yrs.	Cage, box, or hutch	Pellets, greens, grasses, bread, carrots	Very easy
Rat	1–2 lbs.	3–5 yrs.	Same as for mouse, but larger	Seeds, pellets, grasses, greens, table scraps	Easy

Salamander	6"–9"	To 25 yrs.	Terrarium, with water, rocks, earth, twigs	Live: worms, crickets, other insects	Moderate to difficult
Skunk	To 10 lbs.	To 5 yrs.	Large wire cage	Dog food, table scraps, fruits, vegetables	Difficult
Snakes	To 3'	3–6 yrs.	Glass aquarium with wire top	Live: gold-fish, worms, guppies, etc.	Difficult
Tortoise (Land turtle)	1' or more	Same as terrapin	Same as terrapin, but less water	Greens, grasses, dog food, chopped meats	Difficult

SUGGESTED FURTHER READINGS

*Braker, William P. "Know How to Keep Saltwater Fishes." New York: Doubleday.

Caras, Roger. *The Roger Caras Pet Book.* New York: Holt, Rinehart & Winston, 1977.

———. *A Zoo in Your Room.* New York: Harcourt Brace Jovanovich, 1975.

Dolensk, Emil, and Burn, Barbara. *The Penguin Book of Pets: A Practical Guide to Animal Keeping.* Baltimore: Penguin Books, 1978.

Hess, Lilo. *Problem Pets.* New York: Charles Scribner's Sons, 1972.

**Nowinsky, Ira. "Enjoy Your Snakes." New York: Doubleday.

Sabin, Francene, and Sabin, Louis. *Perfect Pets.* New York: G. P. Putnam's Sons, 1978.

Stevens, Carla. *Your First Pet and How to Care for It.* New York: Macmillan, 1974.

*This is part of the "Know How to . . . series of Pet Library booklets. Titles cover a wide range of subjects, such as, *Know Your Aquarium, Know Your Domestic and Exotic Cats, Know How to Breed Tropical Fish,* and so on. They can be purchased in most pet shops.

**This is one of the many booklets in the "Enjoy" series of the Pet Library. There is a booklet for just about any household pet; the titles are available in most pet shops.

INDEX

ABOUT
THE AUTHOR

Stanley Leinwoll has written ten books and hundreds of articles on a wide range of subjects, including a history of radio, a book on candlecrafting, two cookbooks, and book about insurance. Leinwoll has raised at least one of each of the pets discussed in *The Book of Pets* and at present has two dogs, two cats, a pair of parakeets, and a tankful of fish. He is Director of Engineering, United States, for Radio Free Europe and Radio Liberty. He has two grown daughters and lives with his wife, Miriam, near Princeton, New Jersey